THL_ _

A Play In Four Acts

By

JACK LONDON

First published in 1910

British Library Cataloguing-in-Publication Data
A catalogue record for this book is available
from the British Library

CONTENTS

3

JACK LONDON

Jack London was born in San Francisco, USA in 1876. In order to support his working class family, he left school at the age of fourteen and worked in a string of unskilled jobs, before returning briefly to graduate. Around this time, London discovered the public library in Oakland, and immersed himself in the literature of the day. In 1894, after a spell working on merchant ships, he set out to experience the life of the tramp, with a view to gaining an insight into the national class system and the raw essence of the human condition. At the age of nineteen, upon returning, London was admitted to the University of California in Berkeley, but left before graduating after just six months due to financial pressures.

London published his first short story, 'Typhoon off the Coast of Japan', in 1893. At this point, he turned seriously to writing, producing work at a prolific rate. Over the next decade, he began to be published in major magazines of the day, producing some of his best-remembered stories, such as 'To Build a Fire'. Starting in 1902, London turned to novels, producing almost twenty in fifteen years. Of these, his best-known are *Call of the Wild* and *White Fang*, both set during the Klondike Gold Rush. He also produced a number of popular and still widely-anthologized stories, such as 'An Odyssey of the North' and 'Love of Life'. London even proved himself as an excellent journalist, reporting on the 1906 earthquake in San Francisco and the Mexican Revolution of 1910. London was an impassioned advocate of socialism and workers' rights, and these themes inform a number of his works most notably his dystopian novel *The Iron Heel*, published in 1907. He even ran unsuccessfully as the Socialist nominee for mayor of Oakland on two occasions.

London died in 1916, aged 40.

CHARACTERS

MARGARET CHALMERS -
Wife of Senator Chalmers

HOWARD KNOX -
A Congressman from Oregon

THOMAS CHALMERS -
A United States Senator and several times millionaire

MASTER THOMAS CHALMERS -
Son of Margaret and Senator Chalmers

ELLERY JACKSON HUBBARD -
A Journalist

ANTHONY STARKWEATHER -
A great magnate, and father of Margaret Chalmers

MRS STARKWEATHER -
His wife

CONNIE STARKWEATHER -
Their younger daughter

FELIX DOBLEMAN -
Secretary to Anthony Starkweather

LINDA DAVIS -
Maid to Margaret Chalmers

JULIUS RUTLAND -
Episcopalian Minister

JOHN GIEFORD -
Labor Agitator

MATSU SAKARI -
Secretary of Japanese Embassy

DOLORES ORTEGA -
Wife of Peruvian Minister

SENATOR DOWSETT

MRS DOWSETT

HOUSEKEEPER, SERVANTS, AGENTS, ETC

ACTORS' DESCRIPTION
OF CHARACTERS

MARGARET CHALMERS.

Twenty-seven years of age; a strong, mature woman, but quite feminine where her heart or sense of beauty are concerned. Her eyes are wide apart. Has a dazzling smile, which she knows how to use on occasion. Also, on occasion, she can be firm and hard, even cynical An intellectual woman, and at the same time a very womanly woman, capable of sudden tendernesses, flashes of emotion, and abrupt actions. She is a finished product of high culture and refinement, and at the same time possesses robust vitality and instinctive right-promptings that augur well for the future of the race.

HOWARD KNOX.

He might have been a poet, but was turned politician. Inflamed with love for humanity. Thirty-five years of age. He has his vision, and must follow it. He has suffered ostracism because of it, and has followed his vision in spite of abuse and ridicule. Physically, a well-built, powerful man. Strong-featured rather than handsome. Very much in earnest, and, despite his university training, a trifle awkward in carriage and demeanor, lacking in social ease. He has been elected to Congress on a reform ticket, and is almost alone in fight he is making. He has no party to back him, though he has a following of a few independents and insurgents.

THOMAS CHALMERS.

Forty-five to fifty years of age. Iron-gray mustache. Slightly stout. A good liver, much given to Scotch and soda, with a weak heart. Is liable to collapse any time. If anything, slightly lazy or lethargic in his emotional life. One of the "owned" senators representing a decadent New England state, himself master of the state political machine. Also, he is nobody's fool. He possesses the brain and strength of character to play his part. His most distinctive feature is his temperamental opportunism.

MASTER THOMAS CHALMERS.

Six years of age. Sturdy and healthy despite his grandmother's belief to the contrary.

ELLERY JACKSON HUBBARD.

Thirty-eight to forty years of age. Smooth-shaven. A star journalist with a national reputation; a large, heavy-set man, with large head, large hands—everything about him is large. A man radiating prosperity, optimism and selfishness. Has no morality whatever. Is a conscious individualist, cold-blooded, pitiless, working only for himself, and believing in nothing but himself.

ANTHONY STARKWEATHER.

An elderly, well preserved gentleman, slenderly built, showing all the signs of a man who has lived clean and has been almost an ascetic. One to whom the joys of the flesh have had little meaning. A cold, controlled man whose one passion is for power. Distinctively a man of power. An eagle-like man, who, by keenness of brain and force of character, has carved out a fortune of hundreds of millions. In short, an industrial and financial magnate of the first water and of the finest type to be found in the United States. Essentially a moral man, his rigid New England morality has suffered

a sea change and developed into the morality of the master-
man of affairs, equally rigid, equally uncompromising, but
essentially Jesuitical in that he believes in doing wrong that
right may come of it. He is absolutely certain that civilization
and progress rest on his shoulders and upon the shoulders of
the small group of men like him.

MRS. STARKWEATHER.
Of the helpless, comfortably stout, elderly type. She has
not followed her husband in his moral evolution. She is the
creature of old customs, old prejudices, old New England
ethics. She is rather confused by the modern rush of life.

CONNIE STARKWEATHER.
Margaret's younger sister, twenty years old. She is nothing
that Margaret is, and everything that Margaret is not. No
essential evil in her, but has no mind of her own—hopelessly
a creature of convention. Gay, laughing, healthy, buxom—a
natural product of her care-free environment.

FEUX DOBLEMAN.
Private secretary to Anthony Starkweather. A young man
of correct social deportment, thoroughly and in all things
just the sort of private secretary a man like Anthony
Starkweather would have. He is a weak-souled creature,
timorous, almost effeminate.

LINDA DAVIS.
Maid to Margaret. A young woman of twenty-five or so,
blond, Scandinavian, though American-born. A cold woman,
almost featureless because of her long years of training, but
with a hot heart deep down, and characterized by an intense
devotion to her mistress. Wild horses could drag nothing
from her where her mistress is concerned.

JUNUS RUTLAND.

Having no strong features about him, the type realizes itself.

JOHN GIFFORD.

A labor agitator. A man of the people, rough-hewn, narrow as a labor-leader may well be, earnest and sincere. He is a proper, better type of labor-leader.

MATSU SAKARI.

Secretary of Japanese Embassy. He is the perfection of politeness and talks classical book-English. He bows a great deal.

DOLORES ORTEGA.

Wife of Peruvian Minister; bright and vivacious, and uses her hands a great deal as she talks, in the Latin-American fashion.

SENATOR DOWSETT.

Fifty years of age; well preserved.

MRS. DOWSETT.

Stout and middle-aged

ACT I

_____

A ROOM IN THE HOUSE OF SENATOR CHALMERS

Scene. In Senator Chalmers' home. It is four o'clock in
the afternoon, in a modern living room with appropriate
furnishings. In particular, in front, on left, a table prepared for
the serving of tea, all excepting the tea urn itself. At rear, right
of center, is main entrance to the room. Also, doorways at sides,
on left and right. Curtain discloses Chalmers and Hubbard
seated loungingly at the right front.

HUBBARD.
(After an apparent pause for cogitation.) I can't understand
why an old wheel-horse like Elsworth should kick over the
traces that way.

CHALMERS
Disgruntled. Thinks he didn't get his fair share of plums
out of the Tariff Committee. Besides, it's his last term. He's
announced that he's going to retire.

HUBBARD
(Snorting contemptuously, mimicking an old man's pompous
enunciation.) "A Resolution to Investigate the High Cost of
Living!"—old Senator Elsworth introducing a measure like
that! The old buck!—— How are you going to handle it?

13

CHALMERS
It's already handled.

HUBBARD
Yes?

CHALMERS
(Pulling his mustache.) Turned it over to the Committee to
Audit and Control the Contingent Expenses of the Senate.

HUBBARD
(Grinning his appreciation.) And you're chairman. Poor old
Elsworth. This way to the lethal chamber, and the bill's on its
way.

CHALMERS
Elsworth will be retired before it's ever reported. In the
meantime, say after a decent interval, Senator Hodge will
introduce another resolution to investigate the high cost of
living. It will be like Elsworth's, only it won't.

HUBBARD
(Nodding his head and anticipating.) And it will go to the
Committee on Finance and come back for action inside of
twenty-four hours.

CHALMERS
By the way, I see Cartwright's Magazine has ceased muck-
raking.

HUBBARD
Cartwrights never did muck-rake—that is, not the big
Interests—only the small independent businesses that didn't
advertise.

CHALMERS

Yes, it deftly concealed its reactionary tendencies.

HUBBARD

And from now on the concealment will be still more deft. I've gone into it myself. I have a majority of the stock right now.

CHALMERS

I thought I had noticed a subtle change in the last two numbers.

HUBBARD

(Nodding.) We're still going on muck-raking. We have a splendid series on Aged Paupers, demanding better treatment and more sanitary conditions. Also we are going to run "Barbarous Venezuela" and show up thoroughly the rotten political management of that benighted country.

CHALMERS

(Nods approvingly, and, after a pause.) And now concerning Knox. That's what I sent for you about. His speech comes off tomorrow per schedule. At last we've got him where we want him.

HUBBARD

I have the ins and outs of it pretty well. Everything's arranged. The boys have their cue, though they don't know just what's going to be pulled off; and this time to-morrow afternoon their dispatches will be singing along the wires.

CHALMERS

(Firmly and harshly.) This man Knox must be covered with ridicule, swamped with ridicule, annihilated with ridicule.

HUBBARD

It is to laugh. Trust the great American people for that. We'll make those little Western editors sit up. They've been swearing by Knox, like a little tin god. Roars of laughter for them.

CHALMERS

Do you do anything yourself?

HUBBARD

Trust me. I have my own article for Cartwright's blocked out. They're holding the presses for it. I shall wire it along hot-footed to-morrow evening. Say——?

CHALMERS

(After a pause.) Well?

HUBBARD

Wasn't it a risky thing to give him his chance with that speech?

CHALMERS

It was the only feasible thing. He never has given us an opening. Our service men have camped on his trail night and day. Private life as unimpeachable as his public life. But now is our chance. The gods have given him into our hands. That speech will do more to break his influence—

HUBBARD

(Interrupting.) Than a Fairbanks cocktail.

(Both laugh.) But don't forget that this Knox is a live wire. Somebody might get stung. Are you sure, when he gets up to make that speech, that he won't be able to back it up?

CHALMERS
No danger at all.

HUBBARD
But there are hooks and crooks by which facts are sometimes obtained.

CHALMERS
(Positively.) Knox has nothing to go on but suspicions and hints, and unfounded assertions from the yellow press.

(Man-servant enters, goes to tea-table, looks it over, and makes slight rearrangements.) (Lowering his voice.) He will make himself a laughing stock. His charges will turn into boomerangs. His speech will be like a sheet from a Sunday supplement, with not a fact to back it up. (Glances at Servant.) We'd better be getting out of here. They're going to have tea.

(The Servant, however, makes exit.) Come to the library and have a high-ball. (They pause as Hubbard speaks.)

HUBBARD
(With quiet glee.) And to-morrow Ali Baba gets his.

CHALMERS
Ali Baba?

HUBBARD
That's what your wife calls him—Knox.

CHALMERS
Oh, yes, I believe I've heard it before. It's about time he hanged himself, and now we've given him the rope.

HUBBARD

(Sinking voice and becoming deprecatingly confidential.)

Oh, by the way, just a little friendly warning, Senator Chalmers. Not so fast and loose up New York way. That certain lady, not to be mentioned—there's gossip about it in the New York newspaper offices. Of course, all such stories are killed. But be discreet, be discreet If Gherst gets hold of it, he'll play it up against the Administration in all his papers.

(Chalmers, who throughout this speech is showing a growing resentment, is about to speak, when voices are heard without and he checks himself.)

(Enter. Mrs. Starkweather, rather flustered and imminently in danger of a collapse, followed by Connie Starkweather, fresh, radiant, and joyous.)

MRS. STARKWEATHER

(With appeal and relief.)

Oh——Tom!

(Chalmers takes her hand sympathetically and protectingly.)

CONNIE

(Who is an exuberant young woman, bursts forth.) Oh, brother-in-law! Such excitement! That's what's the matter with mother. We ran into a go-cart. Our chauffeur was not to blame. It was the woman's fault. She tried to cross just as we were turning the corner. But we hardly grazed it. Fortunately the baby was not hurt—only spilled. It was ridiculous. (Catching sight of Hubbard.) Oh, there you are, Mr. Hubbard. How de do.

(Steps half way to meet him and shakes hands with him.)
(Mrs. Starkweather looks around helplessly for a chair, and

Chalmers conducts her to one soothingly.)

MRS. STARKWEATHER

Oh, it was terrible! The little child might have been killed.
And such persons love their babies, I know.

CONNIE

(To Chalmers.) Has father come? We were to pick him up
here. Where's Madge?

MRS. STARKWEATHER

(Espying Hubbard, faintly.) Oh, there is Mr. Hubbard.

(Hubbard comes to her and shakes hands.) I simply can't
get used to these rapid ways of modern life. The motor-car
is the invention of the devil. Everything is too quick. When
I was a girl, we lived sedately, decorously. There was time
for meditation and repose. But in this age there is time for
nothing. How Anthony keeps his head is more than I can
understand. But, then, Anthony is a wonderful man.

HUBBARD

I am sure Mr. Starkweather never lost his head in his life.

CHALMERS

Unless when he was courting you, mother.

MRS. STARKWEATHER

(A trifle grimly.) I'm not so sure about that.

CONNIE

(Imitating a grave, business-like enunciation.) Father
probably conferred first with his associates, then turned the
affair over for consideration by his corporation lawyers, and,

when they reported no flaws, checked the first spare half hour in his notebook to ask mother if she would have him.

(They laugh.) And looked at his watch at least twice while he was proposing.

MRS. STARKWEATHER
Anthony was not so busy then as all that.

HUBBARD
He hadn't yet taken up the job of running the United States.

MRS. STARKWEATHER
I'm sure I don't know what he is running, but he is a very busy man—business, politics, and madness; madness, politics, and business.

(She stops breathlessly and glances at tea-table.) Tea. I should like a cup of tea. Connie, I shall stay for a cup of tea, and then, if your father hasn't come, we'll go home. (To Chalmers.) Where is Tommy?

CHALMERS
Out in the car with Madge.

(Glances at tea-table and consults watch.) She should be back now.

CONNIE
Mother, you mustn't stay long. I have to dress.

CHALMERS
Oh, yes, that dinner.

(Yawns.) I wish I could loaf to-night.

CONNIE

(Explaining to Hubbard.) The Turkish Charge d'Affaires—I never can remember his name. But he's great fun—a positive joy. He's giving the dinner to the British Ambassador.

MRS. STARKWEATHER

(Starting forward in her chair and listening intently.) There's Tommy, now.

(Voices of Margaret Chalmers and of Tommy heard from without. Hers is laughingly protesting, while Tommy's is gleefully insistent.) (Margaret and Tommy appear and pause just outside door, holding each other's hands, facing each other, too immersed in each other to be aware of the presence of those inside the room. Margaret and Tommy are in street costume.)

TOMMY

(Laughing.)

But mama.

MARGARET

(Herself laughing, but shaking her head.) No. Tommy First—

MARGARET

No; you must run along to Linda, now, mother's boy. And we'll talk about that some other time.

(Tommy notices for the first time that there are persons in the room. He peeps in around the door and espies Mrs. Starkweather. At the same moment, impulsively, he withdraws his hands and runs in to Mrs. Starkweather.)

TOMMY
(Who is evidently fond of his grandmother.) Grandma!

(They embrace and make much of each other.)

(Margaret enters, appropriately greeting the others—a kiss (maybe) to Connie, and a slightly cold handshake to Hubbard.)

MARGARET
(To Chalmers.) Now that you're here, Tom, you mustn't run away.

(Greets Mrs. Starkweather.)

MRS. STARKWEATHER
(Turning Tommy's face to the light and looking at it anxiously.) A trifle thin, Margaret.

MARGARET
On the contrary, mother——

MRS. STARKWEATHER
(To Chalmers.) Don't you think so, Tom?

CONNIE
(Aside to Hubbard.) Mother continually worries about his health.

HUBBARD
A sturdy youngster, I should say.

TOMMY
(To Chalmers.) I'm an Indian, aren't I, daddy?

CHALMERS
  (Nodding his head emphatically.) And the stoutest-hearted in
  the tribe.

  (Linda appears in doorway, evidently looking for Tommy,
  and Chalmers notices her.) There's Linda looking for you,
  young stout heart.

MARGARET
  Take Tommy, Linda. Run along, mother's boy.

TOMMY
  Come along, grandma. I want to show you something.

  (He catches Mrs. Starkweather by the hand. Protesting,
  but highly pleased, she allows him to lead her to the door,
  where he extends his other hand to Linda. Thus, pausing in
  doorway, leading a woman by either hand, he looks back at
  Margaret.) (Roguishly.) Remember, mama, we're going to
  scout in a little while.

MARGARET
  (Going to Tommy, and bending down with her arms around
  him.) No, Tommy. Mama has to go to that horrid dinner to-
  night. But to-morrow we'll play.

  (Tommy is cast down and looks as if he might pout.) Where
  is my little Indian now?

HUBBARD
  Be an Indian, Tommy.

TOMMY
  (Brightening up.)

All right, mama. To-morrow.——if you can't find time to-day.

(Margaret kisses him.) (Exit Tommy, Mrs. Starkweather, and Linda, Tommy leading them by a hand in each of theirs.)

CHALMERS
(Nodding to Hubbard, in low voice to Hubbard and starting to make exit to right.) That high-ball.

(Hubbard disengages himself from proximity of Connie, and starts to follow.)

CONNIE
(Reproachfully.) If you run away, I won't stop for tea.

MARGARET
Do stop, Tom. Father will be here in a few minutes.

CONNIE
A regular family party.

CHALMERS
All right. We'll be back. We're just going to have a little talk.

(Chalmers and Hubbard make exit to right.) (Margaret puts her arm impulsively around Connie—a sheerly spontaneous act of affection—kisses her, and at same time evinces preparation to leave.)

MARGARET
I've got to get my things off. Won't you wait here, dear, in case anybody comes? It's nearly time.

(Starts toward exit to rear, but is stopped by Connie.) Madge.

(Margaret immediately pauses and waits expectantly, smiling, while Connie is hesitant.)

I want to speak to you about something, Madge. You don't mind?

(Margaret, still smiling, shakes her head.) Just a warning. Not that anybody could believe for a moment, there is anything wrong, but——

MARGARET
(Dispelling a shadow of irritation that has crossed her face.)

If it concerns Tom, don't tell me, please. You know he does do ridiculous things at times. But I don't let him worry me any more; so don't worry me about him.

(Connie remains silent, and Margaret grows curious.) Well?

CONNIE
It's not about Tom—

(Pauses.) It's about you.

MARGARET
Oh.

CONNIE
I don't know how to begin.

MARGARET
By coming right out with it, the worst of it, all at once, first.

CONNIE
It isn't serious at all, but—well, mother is worrying about it. You know how old-fashioned she is. And when you consider

our position—father's and Tom's, I mean—it doesn't seem just right for you to be seeing so much of such an enemy of theirs. He has abused them dreadfully, you know. And there's that dreadful speech he is going to give to-morrow. You haven't seen the afternoon papers. He has made the most terrible charges against everybody—all of us, our friends, everybody.

MARGARET
You mean Mr. Knox, of course. But he wouldn't harm anybody, Connie, dear.

CONNIE
(Bridling,) Oh, he wouldn't? He as good as publicly called father a thief.

MARGARET
When did that happen? I never heard of it.

CONNIE
Well, he said that the money magnates had grown so unprincipled, sunk so low, that they would steal a mouse from a blind kitten.

MARGARET
I don't see what father has to do with that.

CONNIE
He meant him just the same.

MARGARET
You silly goose. He couldn't have meant father. Father? Why, father wouldn't look at anything less than fifty or a hundred millions.

CONNIE

And you speak to him and make much of him when you meet him places. You talked with him for half an hour at that Dugdale reception. You have him here in your own house—Tom's house—when he's such a bitter enemy of Tom's. (During the foregoing speech, Anthony Starkweather makes entrance from rear. His face is grave, and he is in a brown study, as if pondering weighty problems. At sight of the two women he pauses and surveys them. They are unaware of his presence.)

MARGARET

You are wrong, Connie. He is nobody's enemy. He is the truest, cleanest, most right-seeking man I have ever seen.

CONNIE

(Interrupting.) He is a trouble-maker, a disturber of the public peace, a shallow-pated demagogue—

MARGARET

(Reprovingly.)

Now you're quoting somebody—— father, I suppose. To think of him being so abused—poor, dear Ali Baba—

STARKWEATHER

(Clearing his throat in advertisement of his presence.) A-hem.

(Margaret and Connie turn around abruptly and discover him.)

MARGARET

And Connie Father!

(Both come forward to greet him, Margaret leading.)

STARKWEATHER
(Anticipating, showing the deliberate method of the busy man saving time by eliminating the superfluous.) Fine, thank you. Quite well in every particular. This Ali Baba? Who is Ali Baba?

(Margaret looks amused reproach at Connie.)

CONNIE
Mr. Howard Knox.

STARKWEATHER
And why is he called Ali Baba?

MARGARET
That is my nickname for him. In the den of thieves, you know. You remember your Arabian Nights.

STARKWEATHER
(Severely.) I have been wanting to speak to you for some time, Margaret, about that man. You know that I have never interfered with your way of life since your marriage, nor with your and Tom's housekeeping arrangements. But this man Knox. I understand that you have even had him here in your house—

MARGARET
(Interrupting.) He is very liable to be here this afternoon, any time, now.

(Connie displays irritation at Margaret.)

STARKWEATHER

(Continuing imperturbably.) Your house—you, my daughter, and the wife of Senator Chalmers. As I said, I have not interfered with you since your marriage. But this Knox affair transcends household arrangements. It is of political importance. The man is an enemy to our class, a firebrand. Why do you have him here?

MARGARET

Because I like him. Because he is a man I am proud to call "friend." Because I wish there were more men like him, many more men like him, in the world. Because I have ever seen in him nothing but the best and highest. And, besides, it's such good fun to see how one virtuous man can so disconcert you captains of industry and arbiters of destiny. Confess that you are very much disconcerted, father, right now. He will be here in a few minutes, and you will be more disconcerted. Why? Because it is an affair that transcends family arrangements. And it is your affair, not mine.

STARKWEATHER

This man Knox is a dangerous character—one that I am not pleased to see any of my family take up with. He is not a gentleman.

MARGARET

He is a self-made man, if that is what you mean, and he certainly hasn't any money.

CONNIE

(Interrupting.) He says that money is theft—at least when it is in the hands of a wealthy person.

STARKWEATHER

He is uncouth—ignorant.

MARGARET

I happen to know that he is a graduate of the University of Oregon.

STARKWEATHER

(Sneeringly.) A cow college. But that is not what I mean. He is a demagogue, stirring up the wild-beast passions of the people.

MARGARET

Surely you would not call his advocacy of that child labor bill and of the conservation of the forest and coal lands stirring up the wild-beast passions of the people?

STARKWEATHER

(Wearily.) You don't understand. When I say he is dangerous it is because he threatens all the stabilities, because he threatens us who have made this country and upon whom this country and its prosperity rest.

(Connie, scenting trouble, walks across stage away from them.)

MARGARET

The captains of industry—the banking magnates and the mergers?

STARKWEATHER

Call it so. Call it what you will. Without us the country
falls into the hands of scoundrels like that man Knox and
smashes to ruin.

MARGARET

(Reprovingly.) Not a scoundrel, father.

STARKWEATHER

He is a sentimental dreamer, a hair-brained enthusiast. It is
the foolish utterances of men like him that place the bomb
and the knife in the hand of the assassin.

MARGARET

He is at least a good man, even if he does disagree with you
on political and industrial problems. And heaven knows that
good men are rare enough these days.

STARKWEATHER

I impugn neither his morality nor his motives—only his
rationality. Really, Margaret, there is nothing inherently
vicious about him. I grant that. And it is precisely that which
makes him such a power for evil.

MARGARET

When I think of all the misery and pain which he is trying
to remedy—I can see in him only a power for good. He is not
working for himself but for the many. That is why he has no
money. You have heaven alone knows how many millions—
you don't; you have worked for yourself.

STARKWEATHER

I, too, work for the many. I give work to the many. I make life possible for the many. I am only too keenly alive to the responsibilities of my stewardship of wealth.

MARGARET

But what of the child laborers working at the machines? Is that necessary, O steward of wealth? How my heart has ached for them! How I have longed to do something for them—to change conditions so that it will no longer be necessary for the children to toil, to have the playtime of childhood stolen away from them. Theft—that is what it is, the playtime of the children coined into profits. That is why I like Howard Knox. He calls theft theft. He is trying to do something for those children. What are you trying to do for them?

STARKWEATHER

Sentiment. Sentiment. The question is too vast and complicated, and you cannot understand. No woman can understand. That is why you run to sentiment. That is what is the matter with this Knox—sentiment. You can't run a government of ninety millions of people on sentiment, nor on abstract ideas of justice and right.

MARGARET

But if you eliminate justice and right, what remains?

STARKWEATHER

This is a practical world, and it must be managed by practical men—by thinkers, not by near-thinkers whose heads are addled with the half-digested ideas of the French Encyclopedists and Revolutionists of a century and a half ago.

(Margaret shows signs of impatience—she is not particularly perturbed by this passage-at-arms with her father, and is anxious to get off her street things.)

Don't forget, my daughter, that your father knows the books as well as any cow college graduate from Oregon. I, too, in my student days, dabbled in theories of universal happiness and righteousness, saw my vision and dreamed my dream. I did not know then the weakness, and frailty, and grossness of the human clay. But I grew out of that and into a man. Some men never grow out of that stage. That is what is the trouble with Knox. He is still a dreamer, and a dangerous one.

(He pauses a moment, and then his thin lips shut grimly. But he has just about shot his bolt.)

MARGARET

What do you mean?

STARKWEATHER

He has let himself in to give a speech to-morrow, wherein he will be called upon to deliver the proofs of all the lurid charges he has made against the Administration—against us, the stewards of wealth if you please. He will be unable to deliver the proofs, and the nation will laugh. And that will be the political end of Mr. Ali Baba and his dream.

MARGARET

It is a beautiful dream. Were there more like him the dream would come true. After all, it is the dreamers that build and that never die. Perhaps you will find that he is not so easily to be destroyed. But I can't stay and argue with you, father. I simply must go and get my things off.

(To Connie.) You'll have to receive, dear. I'll be right back.

(Julius Rutland enters. Margaret advances to meet him, shaking his hand.) You must forgive me for deserting for a moment.

RUTLAND
(Greeting the others.) A family council, I see.

MARGARET
(On way to exit at rear.) No; a discussion on dreams and dreamers. I leave you to bear my part.

RUTLAND
(Bowing.) With pleasure. The dreamers are the true architects. But—a—what is the dream and who is the dreamer?

MARGARET
(Pausing in the doorway.) The dream of social justice, of fair play and a square deal to everybody. The dreamer—Mr. Knox.

(Rutland is so patently irritated, that Margaret lingers in the doorway to enjoy.)

RUTLAND
That man! He has insulted and reviled the Church—my calling. He—

CONNIE
(Interrupting.) He said the churchmen stole from God. I remember he once said there had been only one true Christian and that He died on the Cross.

MARGARET
He quoted that from Nietzsche.

STARKWEATHER
(To Rutland, in quiet glee.) He had you there.

RUTLAND
(In composed fury.) Nietzsche is a blasphemer, sir. Any man who reads Nietzsche or quotes Nietzsche is a blasphemer. It augurs ill for the future of America when such pernicious literature has the vogue it has.

MARGARET
(Interrupting, laughing.) I leave the quarrel in your hands, sir knight. Remember—the dreamer and the dream. (Margaret makes exit.)

RUTLAND
(Shaking his head.) I cannot understand what is coming over the present generation. Take your daughter, for instance. Ten years ago she was an earnest, sincere lieutenant of mine in all our little charities.

STARKWEATHER
Has she given charity up?

CONNIE
It's settlement work, now, and kindergartens.

RUTLAND
(Ominously.) It's writers like Nietzsche, and men who read him, like Knox, who are responsible.

(Senator Dowsett and Mrs. Dowsett enter from rear.)

(Connie advances to greet them. Rutland knows Mrs. Dowsett, and Connie introduces him to Senator Dowsett.)

(In the meantime, not bothering to greet anybody, evincing his own will and way, Starkweather goes across to right front, selects one of several chairs, seats himself, pulls a thin note-book from inside coat pocket, and proceeds to immerse himself in contents of same.) (Dowsett and Rutland pair and stroll to left rear and seat themselves, while Connie and Mrs. Dowsett seat themselves at tea-table to left front. Connie rings the bell for Servant.)

MRS. DOWSETT
(Glancing significantly at Starkweather, and speaking in a low voice.) That's your father, isn't it? I have so wanted to meet him.

CONNIE
(Softly.) You know he's peculiar. He is liable to ignore everybody here this afternoon, and get up and go away abruptly, without saying good-bye.

MRS. DOWSETT
(Sympathetically.) Yes, I know, a man of such large affairs. He must have so much on his mind. He is a wonderful man—my husband says the greatest in contemporary history—more powerful than a dozen presidents, the King of England, and the Kaiser, all rolled into one.

(Servant enters with tea urn and accessories, and Connie proceeds to serve tea, all accompanied by appropriate patter—"Two lumps?" "One, please." "Lemon;" etc.)

(Rutland and Dowsett come forward to table for their tea, where they remain.)

(Connie, glancing apprehensively across at her father and debating a moment, prepares a cup for him and a small plate with crackers, and hands them to Dowsett, who likewise betrays apprehensiveness.)

CONNIE

Take it to father, please, senator.

(Note:—Throughout the rest of this act, Starkweather is like a being apart, a king sitting on his throne. He divides the tea function with Margaret. Men come up to him and speak with him. He sends for men. They come and go at his bidding. The whole attitude, perhaps unconsciously on his part, is that wherever he may be he is master. This attitude is accepted by all the others; forsooth, he is indeed a great man and master. The only one who is not really afraid of him is Margaret; yet she gives in to him in so far as she lets him do as he pleases at her afternoon tea.) (Dowsett carries the cup of tea and small plate across stage to Starkweather. Starkweather does not notice him at first.)

CONNIE

(Who has been watching.) Tea, father, won't you have a cup of tea?

(Through the following scene between Starkweather and Dowsett, the latter holds cup of tea and crackers, helplessly, at a disadvantage. At the same time Rutland is served with tea and remains at the table, talking with the two women.)

STARKWEATHER

(Looking first at Connie, then peering into cup of tea. He grunts refusal, and for the first time looks up into the other man's face. He immediately closes note-book down on finger to keep the place.) Oh, it's you. Dowsett.

(Painfully endeavoring to be at ease.) A pleasure, Mr. Starkweather, an entirely unexpected pleasure to meet you here. I was not aware you frequented frivolous gatherings of this nature.

STARKWEATHER
(Abruptly and peremptorily.) Why didn't you come when you were sent for this morning?

DOWSETT
I was sick—I was in bed.

STARKWEATHER
That is no excuse, sir. When you are sent for you are to come. Understand? That bill was reported back. Why was it reported back? You told Dobleman you would attend to it.

DOWSETT
It was a slip up. Such things will happen.

STARKWEATHER
What was the matter with that committee? Have you no influence with the Senate crowd? If not, say so, and I'll get some one who has.

DOWSETT
(Angrily.) I refuse to be treated in this manner, Mr. Starkweather. I have some self-respect—

(Starkweather grunts incredulously.) Some decency—

(Starkweather grunts.) A position of prominence in my state. You forget, sir, that in our state organization I occupy no mean place.

STARKWEATHER

(Cutting him off so sharply that Dowsett drops cup and saucer.) Don't you show your teeth to me. I can make you or break you. That state organization of yours belongs to me.

(Dowsett starts—he is learning something new. To hide his feelings, he stoops to pick up cup and saucer.) Let it alone! I am talking to you.

(Dowsett straightens up to attention with alacrity.) (Connie, who has witnessed, rings for Servant.) I bought that state organization, and paid for it. You are one of the chattels that came along with the machine. You were made senator to obey my orders. Understand? Do you understand?

DOWSETT

(Beaten.) I—I understand.

STARKWEATHER

That bill is to be killed.

DOWSETT

Yes, sir.

STARKWEATHER

Quietly, no headlines about it.

(Dowsett nods.) Now you can go.

(Dowsett proceeds rather limply across to join group at tea-table.) (Chalmers and Hubbard enter from right, laughing about something. At sight of Starkweather they immediately become sober.) (No hands are shaken. Starkweather barely acknowledges Hubbard's greeting.)

STARKWEATHER

Tom, I want to see you.

(Hubbard takes his cue, and proceeds across to tea-table.)

(Enter Servant. Connie directs him to remove broken cup and saucer. While this is being done, Starkweather remains silent. He consults note-book, and Chalmers stands, not quite at ease, waiting the other's will. At the same time, patter at tea-table. Hubbard, greeting others and accepting or declining cup of tea.)

(Servant makes exit).

STARKWEATHER

(Closing finger on book and looking sharply at Chalmers.) Tom, this affair of yours in New York must come to an end. Understand?

CHALMERS

(Starting.) Hubbard has been talking.

STARKWEATHER

No, it is not Hubbard. I have the reports from other sources.

CHALMERS

It is a harmless affair.

STARKWEATHER

I happen to know better. I have the whole record. If you wish, I can give you every detail, every meeting. I know. There is no discussion whatever. I want no more of it.

CHALMERS

I never dreamed for a moment that I was—er—indiscreet.

STARKWEATHER

Never forget that every indiscretion of a man in your
position is indiscreet. We have a duty, a great and solemn
duty to perform. Upon our shoulders rest the destinies of
ninety million people. If we fail in our duty, they go down to
destruction. Ignorant demagogues are working on the beast-
passions of the people. If they have their way, they are lost,
the country is lost, civilization is lost. We want no more Dark
Ages.

CHALMERS

Really, I never thought it was as serious as all that.

STARKWEATHER

(Shrugging shoulders and lifting eyebrows.) After all, why
should you? You are only a cog in the machine. I, and the
several men grouped with me, am the machine. You are a
useful cog—too useful to lose—

CHALMERS

Lose?—Me?

STARKWEATHER

I have but to raise my hand, any time—do you understand?—
any time, and you are lost. You control your state. Very well.
But never forget that to-morrow, if I wished, I could buy
your whole machine out from under you. I know you cannot
change yourself, but, for the sake of the big issues at stake,
you must be careful, exceedingly careful. We are compelled
to work with weak tools. You are a good liver, a flesh-pot
man. You drink too much. Your heart is weak.—Oh, I have

41

the report of your doctor. Nevertheless, don't make a fool of yourself, nor of us. Besides, do not forget that your wife is my daughter. She is a strong woman, a credit to both of us. Be careful that you are not a discredit to her.

CHALMERS

All right, I'll be careful. But while we are—er—on this subject, there's something I'd like to speak to you about.

(A pause, in which Starkweather waits non-committally.) It's this man Knox, and Madge. He comes to the house. They are as thick as thieves.

STARKWEATHER

Yes?

CHALMERS

(Hastily.) Oh, not a breath of suspicion or anything of that sort, I assure you. But it doesn't strike me as exactly appropriate that your daughter and my wife should be friendly with this fire-eating anarchist who is always attacking us and all that we represent.

STARKWEATHER

I started to speak with her on that subject, but was interrupted.

(Puckers brow and thinks.) You are her husband. Why don't you take her in hand yourself?

(Enters Mrs. Starkweather from rear, looking about, bowing, then locating Starkweather and proceeding toward him.)

CHALMERS

What can I do? She has a will of her own—the same sort of a will that you have. Besides, I think she knows about my—about some of my—indiscretions.

STARKWEATHER

(Slyly.)

Harmless indiscretions?

(Chalmers is about to reply, but observes Mrs. Starkweather approaching.)

MRS. STARKWEATHER

(Speaks in a peevish, complaining voice, and during her harrangue Starkweather immerses himself in notebook.) Oh, there you are, Anthony. Talking politics, I suppose. Well, as soon as I get a cup of tea we must go. Tommy is not looking as well as I could wish. Margaret loves him, but she does not take the right care of him. I don't know what the world is coming to when mothers do not know how to rear their offspring. There is Margaret, with her slum kindergartens, taking care of everybody else's children but her own. If she only performed her church duties as eagerly! Mr. Rutland is displeased with her. I shall give her a talking to—only, you'd better do it, Anthony. Somehow, I have never counted much with Margaret. She is as set in doing what she pleases as you are. In my time children paid respect to their parents. This is what comes of speed. There is no time for anything. And now I must get my tea and run. Connie has to dress for that dinner.

(Mrs. Starkweather crosses to table, greets others characteristically and is served with tea by Connie.)

(Chalmers waits respectfully on Starkweather.)

STARKWEATHER

(Looking up from note-book.) That will do, Tom.

(Chalmers is just starting across to join others, when voices are heard outside rear entrance, and Margaret enters with Dolores Ortega, wife of the Peruvian Minister, and Matsu Sakari, Secretary of Japanese Legation—both of whom she has met as they were entering the house.)

(Chalmers changes his course, and meets the above advancing group. He knows Dolores Ortega, whom he greets, and is introduced to Sakari.)

(Margaret passes on among guests, greeting them, etc. Then she displaces Connie at tea-table and proceeds to dispense tea to the newcomers.)

(Groups slowly form and seat themselves about stage as follows: Chalmers and Dolores Ortega; Rutland, Dowsett, Mrs. Starkweather; Connie, Mr. Dowsett, and Hubbard.)

(Chalmers carries tea to Dolores Ortega.)

(Sakari has been lingering by table, waiting for tea and pattering with Margaret, Chalmers, etc.)

MARGARET

(Handing cup to Sakari.) I am very timid in offering you this, for I am sure you must be appalled by our barbarous methods of making tea.

SAKARI

(Bowing.) It is true, your American tea, and the tea of the English, are quite radically different from the tea in my country. But one learns, you know. I served my apprenticeship to American tea long years ago, when I was at Yale. It was perplexing, I assure you—at first, only at first I

44

really believe that I am beginning to have a—how shall I call it?—a tolerance for tea in your fashion.

MARGARET
You are very kind in overlooking our shortcomings.

SAKARI
(Bowing.) On the contrary, I am unaware, always unaware, of any shortcomings of this marvelous country of yours.

MARGARET
(Laughing.) You are incorrigibly gracious, Mr. Sakari. (Knox appears at threshold of rear entrance and pauses irresolutely for a moment)

SAKARI
(Noticing Knox, and looking about him to select which group he will join.) If I may be allowed, I shall now retire and consume this—tea.

(Joins group composed of Connie, Mrs. Dowsett, and Hubbard.)

(Knox comes forward to Margaret, betraying a certain awkwardness due to lack of experience in such social functions. He greets Margaret and those in the group nearest her.)

KNOX
(To Margaret.) I don't know why I come here. I do not belong. All the ways are strange.

MARGARET
(Lightly, at the same time preparing his tea.) The same Ali Baba—once again in the den of the forty thieves. But your

watch and pocket-book are safe here, really they are.

(Knox makes a gesture of dissent at her facetiousness.) Now don't be serious. You should relax sometimes. You live too tensely.

(Looking at Starkweather.) There's the arch-anarch over there, the dragon you are trying to slay.

(Knox looks at Starkweather and is plainly perplexed.) The man who handles all the life insurance funds, who controls more strings of banks and trust companies than all the Rothschilds a hundred times over—the merger of iron and steel and coal and shipping and all the other things—the man who blocks your child labor bill and all the rest of the remedial legislation you advocate. In short, my father.

KNOX
(Looking intently at Starkweather.) I should have recognized him from his photographs. But why do you say such things?

MARGARET
Because they are true.

(He remains silent.) Now, aren't they? (She laughs.) Oh, you don't need to answer. You know the truth, the whole bitter truth. This is a den of thieves. There is Mr. Hubbard over there, for instance, the trusty journalist lieutenant of the corporations.

KNOX
(With an expression of disgust.) I know him. It was he that wrote the Standard Oil side of the story, after having abused Standard Oil for years in the pseudo-muck-raking magazines. He made them come up to his price, that was all. He's the star writer on Cartwright's, now, since that magazine

changed its policy and became subsidizedly reactionary. I know him—a thoroughly dishonest man. Truly am I Ali Baba, and truly I wonder why I am here.

MARGARET

You are here, sir, because I like you to come.

KNOX

We do have much in common, you and I.

MARGARET

The future.

KNOX

(Gravely, looking at her with shining eyes.) I sometimes fear for more immediate reasons than that.

(Margaret looks at him in alarm, and at the same time betrays pleasure in what he has said.) For you.

MARGARET

(Hastily.) Don't look at me that way. Your eyes are flashing. Some one might see and misunderstand.

KNOX

(In confusion, awkwardly.) I was unaware that I—that I was looking at you——in any way that——

MARGARET

I'll tell you why you are here. Because I sent for you.

KNOX

(With signs of ardor.) I would come whenever you sent for me, and go wherever you might send me.

MARGARET
(Reprovingly.)

Please, please—— It was about that speech. I have been
hearing about it from everybody—rumblings and mutterings
and dire prophecies. I know how busy you are, and I ought
not to have asked you to come. But there was no other way,
and I was so anxious.

KNOX
(Pleased.) It seems so strange that you, being what you are,
affiliated as you are, should be interested in the welfare of the
common people.

MARGARET
(Judicially.) I do seem like a traitor in my own camp. But as
father said a while ago, I, too, have dreamed my dream. I did
it as a girl—Plato's Republic, Moore's Utopia—I was steeped
in all the dreams of the social dreamers.

(During all that follows of her speech, Knox is keenly
interested, his eyes glisten and he hangs on her words.)

And I dreamed that I, too, might do something to bring
on the era of universal justice and fair play. In my heart I
dedicated myself to the cause of humanity. I made Lincoln
my hero-he still is. But I was only a girl, and where was I
to find this cause?—how to work for it? I was shut in by a
thousand restrictions, hedged in by a thousand conventions.
Everybody laughed at me when I expressed the thoughts
that burned in me. What could I do? I was only a woman. I
had neither vote nor right of utterance. I must remain silent.
I must do nothing. Men, in their lordly wisdom, did all.
They voted, orated, governed. The place for women was in
the home, taking care of some lordly man who did all these
lordly things.

KNOX

You understand, then, why I am for equal suffrage.

MARGARET

But I learned—or thought I learned. Power, I discovered
early. My father had power. He was a magnate—I believe that
is the correct phrase. Power was what I needed. But how?
I was a woman. Again I dreamed my dream—a modified
dream. Only by marriage could I win to power. And there
you have the clew to me and what I am and have become.
I met the man who was to become my husband. He was
clean and strong and an athlete, an outdoor man, a wealthy
man and a rising politician. Father told me that if I married
him he would make him the power of his state, make him
governor, send him to the United States Senate. And there
you have it all.

KNOX

Yes?—— Yes?

MARGARET

I married. I found that there were greater forces at work than
I had ever dreamed of. They took my husband away from me
and molded him into the political lieutenant of my father.
And I was without power. I could do nothing for the cause.
I was beaten. Then it was that I got a new vision. The future
belonged to the children. There I could play my woman's
part. I was a mother. Very well. I could do no better than
to bring into the world a healthy son and bring him up to
manhood healthy and wholesome, clean, noble, and alive.
Did I do my part well, through him the results would be
achieved. Through him would the work of the world be done
in making the world healthier and happier for all the human
creatures in it. I played the mother's part. That is why I left
the pitiful little charities of the church and devoted myself

to settlement work and tenement house reform, established my kindergartens, and worked for the little men and women who come so blindly and to whom the future belongs to make or mar.

KNOX

You are magnificent. I know, now, why I come when you bid me come.

MARGARET

And then you came. You were magnificent. You were my knight of the windmills, tilting against all power and privilege, striving to wrest the future from the future and realize it here in the present, now. I was sure you would be destroyed. Yet you are still here and fighting valiantly. And that speech of yours to-morrow—

CHALMERS

(Who has approached, bearing Dolores Ortega's cup.) Yes, that speech. How do you do, Mr. Knox.

(They shake hands.) A cup of tea, Madge. For Mrs. Ortega. Two lumps, please.

(Margaret prepares the cup of tea.) Everybody is excited over that speech. You are going to give us particular fits, to-morrow, I understand.

KNOX

(Smiling.) Really, no more than is deserved.

CHALMERS

The truth, the whole truth, and nothing but the truth?

KNOX

Precisely.

(Receiving back cup of tea from Margaret.)

CHALMERS

Believe me, we are not so black as we're painted. There are two sides to this question. Like you, we do our best to do what is right. And we hope, we still hope, to win you over to our side.

(Knox shakes his head with a quiet smile.)

MARGARET

Oh, Tom, be truthful. You don't hope anything of the sort. You know you are hoping to destroy him.

CHALMERS

(Smiling grimly.) That is what usually happens to those who are not won over.

(Preparing to depart with cup of tea; speaking to Knox.) You might accomplish much good, were you with us. Against us you accomplish nothing, absolutely nothing.

(Returns to Dolores Ortega.)

MARGARET

(Hurriedly.) You see. That is why I was anxious—why I sent for you. Even Tom admits that they who are not won over are destroyed. This speech is a crucial event. You know how rigidly they rule the House and gag men like you. It is they, and they alone, who have given you opportunity for this speech? Why?—Why?

KNOX

(Smiling confidently.) I know their little scheme. They have heard my charges. They think I am going to make a firebrand speech, and they are ready to catch me without the proofs. They are ready in every way for me. They are going to laugh me down. The Associated Press, the Washington correspondents—all are ready to manufacture, in every newspaper in the land, the great laugh that will destroy me. But I am fully prepared, I have—

MARGARET

The proofs?

KNOX

Yes.

MARGARET

Now?

KNOX

They will be delivered to me to-night—original documents, photographs of documents, affidavits—

MARGARET

Tell me nothing. But oh, do be careful! Be careful!

MRS. DOWSETT

(Appealing to Margaret.) Do give me some assistance, Mrs. Chalmers.

(Indicating Sakari.) Mr. Sakari is trying to make me ridiculous.

MARGARET
Impossible.

MRS. DOWSETT
But he is. He has had the effrontery—

CHALMERS
(Mimicking Mrs. Dowsett.) Effrontery!—O, Sakari!

SAKARI
The dear lady is pleased to be facetious.

MRS. DOWSETT
He has had the effrontery to ask me to explain the cause of high prices. Mr. Dowsett says the reason is that the people are living so high.

SAKARI
Such a marvelous country. They are poor because they have so much to spend.

CHALMERS
Are not high prices due to the increased output of gold?

MRS. DOWSETT
Mr. Sakari suggested that himself, and when I agreed with him he proceeded to demolish it. He has treated me dreadfully.

RUTLAND
(Clearing his throat and expressing himself with ponderous unction.) You will find the solution in the drink traffic. It is liquor, alcohol, that is undermining our industry, our

institutions, our faith in God—everything. Yearly the working people drink greater quantities of alcohol. Naturally, through resulting inefficiency, the cost of production is higher, and therefore prices are higher.

DOWSETT

Partly so, partly so. And in line with it, and in addition to it, prices are high because the working class is no longer thrifty. If our working class saved as the French peasant does, we would sell more in the world market and have better times.

SAKARI

(Bowing.) As I understand it then, the more thrifty you are the more you save, and the more you save the more you have to sell, the more you sell, the better the times?

DOWSETT

Exactly so. Exactly.

SAKARI

The less you sell, the harder are the times?

DOWSETT

Just so.

SAKARI

Then if the people are thrifty, and buy less, times will be harder?

DOWSETT

(Perplexed.) Er—it would seem so.

SAKARI

Then it would seem that the present bad times are due to the fact that the people are thrifty, rather than not thrifty?

(Dowsett is nonplussed, and Mrs. Dowsett throws up her hands in despair.)

MRS. DOWSETT

(Turning to Knox.) Perhaps you can explain to us, Mr. Knox, the reason for this terrible condition of affairs.

(Starkweather closes note-book on finger and listens.) (Knox smiles, but does not speak.)

DOLORES ORTEGA

Please do, Mr. Knox. I am so dreadfully anxious to know why living is so high now. Only this morning I understand meat went up again.

(Knox hesitates and looks questioningly at Margaret.)

HUBBARD

I am sure Mr. Knox can shed new light on this perplexing problem.

CHALMERS

Surely you, the whirlwind of oratorical swords in the House, are not timid here—among friends.

KNOX

(Sparring.) I had no idea that questions of such nature were topics of conversation at affairs like this.

STARKWEATHER

(Abruptly and imperatively.) What causes the high prices?

KNOX

(Equally abrupt and just as positive as the other was imperative.) Theft!

(It is a sort of a bombshell he has exploded, but they receive it politely and smilingly, even though it has shaken them up.)

DOLORES ORTEGA

What a romantic explanation. I suppose everybody who has anything has stolen it.

KNOX

Not quite, but almost quite. Take motorcars, for example. This year five hundred million dollars has been spent for motor-cars. It required men toiling in the mines and foundries, women sewing their eyes out in sweat-shops, shop girls slaving for four and five dollars a week, little children working in the factories and cotton-mills—all these it required to produce those five hundred millions spent this year in motor-cars. And all this has been stolen from those who did the work.

MRS. STARKWEATHER

I always knew those motor-cars were to blame for terrible things.

DOLORES ORTEGA

But Mr. Knox, I have a motor-car.

KNOX

Somebody's labor made that car. Was it yours?

DOLORES ORTEGA

Mercy, no! I bought it—— and paid for it.

KNOX
Then did you labor at producing something else, and exchange the fruits of that labor for the motor-car?

(A pause.)

You do not answer. Then I am to understand that you have a motor-car which was made by somebody else's labor and for which you gave no labor of your own. This I call theft. You call it property. Yet it is theft.

STARKWEATHER
(Interrupting Dolores Ortega who was just about to speak.)

But surely you have intelligence to see the question in larger ways than stolen motor-cars. I am a man of affairs. I don't steal motor-cars.

KNOX
(Smiling.) Not concrete little motor-cars, no. You do things on a large scale.

STARKWEATHER
Steal?

KNOX
(Shrugging his shoulders.) If you will have it so.

STARKWEATHER
I am like a certain gentleman from Missouri. You've got to show me.

KNOX
And I'm like the man from Texas. It's got to be put in my hand.

STARKWEATHER

I shift my residence at once to Texas. Put it in my hand that I steal on a large scale.

KNOX

Very well. You are the great financier, merger, and magnate. Do you mind a few statistics?

STARKWEATHER

Go ahead.

KNOX

You exercise a controlling interest in nine billion dollars' worth of railways; in two billion dollars' worth of industrial concerns; in one billion dollars' worth of life insurance groups; in one billion dollars' worth of banking groups; in two billion dollars' worth of trust companies. Mind you, I do not say you own all this, but that you exercise a controlling interest. That is all that is necessary. In short, you exercise a controlling interest in such a proportion of the total investments of the United States, as to set the pace for all the rest. Now to my point. In the last few years seventy billions of dollars have been artificially added to the capitalization of the nation's industries. By that I mean water—pure, unadulterated water. You, the merger, know what water means. I say seventy billions. It doesn't matter if we call it forty billions or eighty billions; the amount, whatever it is, is a huge one. And what does seventy billions of water mean? It means, at five per cent, that three billions and a half must be paid for things this year, and every year, more than things are really worth. The people who labor have to pay this. There is theft for you. There is high prices for you. Who put in the water? Who gets the theft of the water? Have I put it in your hand?

STARKWEATHER

Are there no wages for stewardship?

KNOX

Call it any name you please.

STARKWEATHER

Do I not make two dollars where one was before? Do I not make for more happiness than was before I came?

KNOX

Is that any more than the duty any man owes to his fellowman?

STARKWEATHER

Oh, you unpractical dreamer. (Returns to his note-book.)

RUTLAND

(Throwing himself into the breach.) Where do I steal, Mr. Knox?—I who get a mere salary for preaching the Lord's Word.

KNOX

Your salary comes out of that water I mentioned. Do you want to know who pays your salary? Not your parishioners. But the little children toiling in the mills, and all the rest—all the slaves on the wheel of labor pay you your salary.

RUTLAND

I earn it.

KNOX

They pay it.

MRS. DOWSETT

Why, I declare, Mr. Knox, you are worse than Mr. Sakari.
You are an anarchist.

(She simulates shivering with fear.)

CHALMERS

(To Knox.) I suppose that's part of your speech to-morrow.

DOLORES ORTEGA

(Clapping her hands.) A rehearsal! He's trying it out on us!

SAKARI

How would you remedy this—er—this theft?

(Starkweather again closes note-book on finger and listens as
Knox begins to speak.)

KNOX

Very simply. By changing the governmental machinery by
which this household of ninety millions of people conducts
its affairs.

SAKARI

I thought—I was taught so at Yale—that your governmental
machinery was excellent, most excellent.

KNOX

It is antiquated. It is ready for the scrap-heap. Instead of
being our servant, it has mastered us. We are its slaves. All
the political brood of grafters and hypocrites have run away
with it, and with us as well. In short, from the municipalities
up, we are dominated by the grafters. It is a reign of theft.

HUBBARD

But any government is representative of its people. No people is worthy of a better government than it possesses. Were it worthier, it would possess a better government.

(Starkweather nods his head approvingly.)

KNOX

That is a lie. And I say to you now that the average morality and desire for right conduct of the people of the United States is far higher than that of the government which misrepresents it. The people are essentially worthy of a better government than that which is at present in the hands of the politicians, for the benefit of the politicians and of the interests the politicians represent. I wonder, Mr. Sakari, if you have ever heard the story of the four aces.

SAKARI

I cannot say that I have.

KNOX

Do you understand the game of poker?

SAKARI

(Considering.) Yes, a marvelous game. I have learned it—at Yale. It was very expensive.

KNOX

Well, that story reminds me of our grafting politicians. They have no moral compunctions. They look upon theft as right—eminently right. They see nothing wrong in the arrangement that the man who deals the cards should give himself the best in the deck. Never mind what he deals himself, they'll have the deal next and make up for it.

DOLORES ORTEGA

But the story, Mr. Knox. I, too, understand poker.

KNOX

It occurred out in Nevada, in a mining camp. A tenderfoot was watching a game of poker, He stood behind the dealer, and he saw the dealer deal himself four aces from the bottom of the deck.

(From now on, he tells the story in the slow, slightly drawling Western fashion.) The tenderfoot went around to the player on the opposite side of the table.

"Say," he says, "I just seen the dealer give himself four aces off the bottom."

The player looked at him a moment, and said, "What of it?"

"Oh, nothing," said the tenderfoot, "only I thought you might want to know. I tell you I seen the dealer give himself four aces off the bottom."

"Look here, Mister," said the player, "you'd better get out of this. You don't understand the game. It's HIS deal, ain't it?"

MARGARET

(Arising while they are laughing.) We've talked politics long enough. Dolores, I want you to tell me about your new car.

KNOX

(As if suddenly recollecting himself.) And I must be going.

(In a low voice to Margaret.) Do I have to shake hands with all these people?

MARGARET

(Shaking her head, speaking low.) Dear delightful Ali Baba.

KNOX

(Glumly.) I suppose I've made a fool of myself.

MARGARET

(Earnestly.) On the contrary, you were delightful. I am proud of you.

(As Knox shakes hands with Margaret, Sakari arises and comes forward).

SAKARI

I, too, must go. I have had a charming half hour, Mrs. Chalmers. But I shall not attempt to thank you.

(He shakes hands with Margaret.)

(Knox and Sakari proceed to make exit to rear.)

(Just as they go out, Servant enters, carrying card-tray, and advances toward Starkweather.)

(Margaret joins Dolores Ortega and Chalmers, seats herself with them, and proceeds to talk motor-cars.)

(Servant has reached Starkweather, who has taken a telegram from tray, opened it, and is reading it.)

STARKWEATHER

Damnation!

SERVANT

I beg your pardon, sir.

STARKWEATHER

Send Senator Chalmers to me, and Mr. Hubbard.

SERVANT
Yes, sir.

(Servant crosses to Chalmers and Hubbard, both of whom immediately arise and cross to Starkweather.)

(While this is being done, Margaret reassembles the three broken groups into one, seating herself so that she can watch Starkweather and his group across the stage.)

(Servant lingers to receive a command from Margaret.)

(Chalmers and Hubbard wait a moment, standing, while Starkweather rereads telegram.)

STARKWEATHER
(Standing up.) Dobleman has just forwarded this telegram. It's from New York—from Martinaw. There's been rottenness. My papers and letter-files have been ransacked. It's the confidential stenographer who has been tampered with—you remember that middle-aged, youngish-oldish woman, Tom? That's the one.—Where's that servant?

(Servant is just making exit.) Here! Come here!

(Servant comes over to Starkweather.) Go to the telephone and call up Dobleman. Tell him to come here.

SERVANT
(Perplexed.) I beg pardon, sir.

STARKWEATHER
(Irritably.) My secretary. At my house. Dobleman. Tell him to come at once.

(Servant makes exit.)

CHALMERS

But who can be the principal behind this theft?

(Starkweather shrugs his shoulders.)

HUBBARD

A blackmailing device most probably. They will attempt to bleed you—

CHALMERS

Unless—

STARKWEATHER

(Impatiently.) Yes?

CHALMERS

Unless they are to be used to-morrow in that speech of Knox.

(Comprehension dawns on the faces of the other two men.)

MRS. STARKWEATHER

(Who has arisen.) Anthony, we must go now. Are you ready? Connie has to dress.

STARKWEATHER

I am not going now. You and Connie take the car.

MRS. STARKWEATHER

You mustn't forget you are going to that dinner.

STARKWEATHER

(Wearily.) Do I ever forget?

(Servant enters and proceeds toward Starkweather, where he stands waiting while Mrs. Starkweather finishes the next speech. Starkweather listens to her with a patient, stony face.)

MRS. STARKWEATHER

Oh, these everlasting politics! That is what it has been all afternoon—high prices, graft, and theft; theft, graft, and high prices. It is terrible. When I was a girl we did not talk of such things. Well, come on, Connie.

MRS. DOWSETT

(Rising and glancing at Dowsett.) And we must be going, too.

(During the following scene, which takes place around Starkweather, Margaret is saying good-bye to her departing guests.)

(Mrs. Starkweather and Connie make exit.)

(Dowsett and Mrs. Dowsett make exit.)

(The instant Mrs. Dowsett's remark puts a complete end to Mrs. Starkweather's speech, Starkweather, without answer or noticing his wife, turns and interrogates Servant with a glance.)

SERVANT

Mr. Dobleman has already left some time to come here, sir.

STARKWEATHER

Show him in as soon as he comes.

SERVANT

Yes, sir.

(Servant makes exit.)

(Margaret, Dolores Ortega, and Rutland are left in a group together, this time around tea-table, where Margaret serves Rutland another cup of tea. From time to time Margaret glances curiously at the serious group of men across the stage.)

(Starkweather is thinking hard with knitted brows. Hubbard is likewise pondering.)

CHALMERS

If I were certain Knox had those papers I would take him by the throat and shake them out of him.

STARKWEATHER

No foolish talk like that, Tom. This is a serious matter.

HUBBARD

But Knox has no money. A Starkweather stenographer comes high.

STARKWEATHER

There is more than Knox behind this. (Enter Dobleman, walking quickly and in a state of controlled excitement.)

DOBLEMAN

(To Starkweather.) You received that telegram, sir?

(Starkweather nods.) I got the New York office—Martinaw— right along afterward, by long distance. I thought best to follow and tell you.

STARKWEATHER

What did Martinaw say?

DOBLEMAN
The files seem in perfect order.

STARKWEATHER
Thank God!

(During the following speech of Dobleman, Rutland says good-bye to Margaret and Dolores Ortega and makes exit.)

(Margaret and Dolores Ortega rise a minute afterward and go toward exit, throwing curious glances at the men but not disturbing them.)

(Dolores Ortega makes exit.)

(Margaret pauses in doorway a moment, giving a final anxious glance at the men, and makes exit.)

DOBLEMAN
But they are not. The stenographer, Miss Standish, has confessed. For a long time she has followed the practice of taking two or three letters and documents at a time away from the office. Many have been photographed and returned. But the more important ones were retained and clever copies returned. Martinaw says that Miss Standish herself does not know and cannot tell which of the ones she returned are genuine and which are copies.

HUBBARD
Knox never did this.

STARKWEATHER
Did Martinaw say whom Miss Standish was acting for?

DOBLEMAN
Gherst.

(The alarm on the three men's faces is patent.)

STARKWEATHER

Gherst!

(Pauses to think.)

HUBBARD

Then it is not so grave after all. A yellow journal sensation is the best Gherst can make of it. And, documents or not, the very medium by which it is made public discredits it.

STARKWEATHER

Trust Gherst for more ability than that. He will certainly exploit them in his newspapers, but not until after Knox has used them in his speech. Oh, the cunning dog! Never could he have chosen a better mode and moment to strike at me, at the Administration, at everything. That is Gherst all over. Playing to the gallery. Inducing Knox to make this spectacular exposure on the floor of the House just at the critical time when so many important bills are pending.

(To Dobleman.)

Did Martinaw give you any idea of the nature of the stolen documents?

DOBLEMAN

(Referring to notes he has brought.) Of course I don't know anything about it, but he spoke of the Goodyear letters—

(Starkweather betrays by his face the gravity of the information.)

the Caledonian letters, all the Black Rider correspondence. He mentioned, too, (Referring to notes.) the Astonbury and Glutz letters. And there were others, many others, not designated.

STARKWEATHER

This is terrible!

(Recollecting himself.)

Thank you, Dobleman. Will you please return to the house at once. Get New York again, and fullest details. I'll follow you shortly. Have you a machine?

DOBLEMAN

A taxi, sir.

STARKWEATHER

All right, and be careful.

(Dobleman makes exit)

CHALMERS

I don't know the import of all these letters, but I can guess, and it does seem serious.

STARKWEATHER

(Furiously.) Serious! Let me tell you that there has been no exposure like this in the history of the country. It means hundreds of millions of dollars. It means more—the loss of power. And still more, it means the mob, the great mass of the child-minded people rising up and destroying all that I have labored to do for them. Oh, the fools! The fools!

HUBBARD

(Shaking his head ominously.) There is no telling what may happen if Knox makes that speech and delivers the proofs.

CHALMERS

It is unfortunate. The people are restless and excited as it is. They are being constantly prodded on by the mouthings of the radical press, of the muck-raking magazines and of the demagogues. The people are like powder awaiting the spark.

STARKWEATHER

This man Knox is no fool, if he is a dreamer. He is a shrewd knave. He is a fighter. He comes from the West—the old pioneer stock. His father drove an ox-team across the Plains to Oregon. He knows how to play his cards, and never could circumstances have placed more advantageous cards in his hands.

CHALMERS

And nothing like this has ever touched you before.

STARKWEATHER

I have always stood above the muck and ruck—clear and clean and unassailable. But this—this is too much! It is the spark. There is no forecasting what it may develop into.

CHALMERS

A political turnover.

STARKWEATHER

(Nodding savagely.) A new party, a party of demagogues, in power. Government ownership of the railways and telegraphs. A graduated income tax that will mean no less than the confiscation of private capital.

CHALMERS

And all that mass of radical legislation—the Child Labor Bill, the new Employers' Liability Act, the government control of the Alaskan coal fields, that interference with Mexico. And that big power corporation you have worked so hard to form.

STARKWEATHER

It must not be. It is an unthinkable calamity. It means that the very process of capitalistic development is hindered, stopped. It means a setback of ten years in the process. It means work, endless work, to overcome the setback. It means not alone the passage of all this radical legislation with the consequent disadvantages, but it means the fingers of the mob clutching at our grip of control. It means anarchy. It means ruin and misery for all the blind fools and led-cattle of the mass who will strike at the very sources of their own existence and comfort.

(Tommy enters from left, evidently playing a game, in the course of which he is running away. By his actions he shows that he is pursued. He intends to cross stage, but is stopped by sight of the men. Unobserved by them, he retraces his steps and crawls under the tea-table.)

CHALMERS

Without doubt, Knox is in possession of the letters right now.

STARKWEATHER

There is but one thing to do, and that is—get them back.

(He looks questioningly at the two men.)

(Margaret enters from left, in flushed and happy pursuit of Tommy—for it is a game she is playing with him. She startles at sight of the three men, whom she first sees as she gains the side of the tea-table, where she pauses abruptly, resting one hand on the table.)

HUBBARD

I'll undertake it.

STARKWEATHER

There is little time to waste. In twenty hours from now he will be on the floor making his speech. Try mild measures first. Offer him inducements—any inducement. I empower you to act for me. You will find he has a price.

HUBBARD

And if not?

STARKWEATHER

Then you must get them at any cost.

HUBBARD

(Tentatively.) You mean—?

STARKWEATHER

I mean just that. But no matter what happens, I must never be brought in. Do you understand?

HUBBARD

Thoroughly.

MARGARET

(Acting her part, and speaking with assumed gayety.) What are you three conspiring about? (All three men are startled.)

CHALMERS

We are arranging to boost prices a little higher.

HUBBARD
And so be able to accumulate more motorcars.

STARKWEATHER
(Taking no notice of Margaret and starting toward exit to rear.) I must be going. Hubbard, you have your work cut out for you. Tom, I want you to come with me.

CHALMERS
(As the three men move toward exit.) Home?

STARKWEATHER
Yes, we have much to do.

CHALMERS
Then I'll dress first and follow you.

(Turning to Margaret.) Pick me up on the way to that dinner.

(Margaret nods. Starkweather makes exit without speaking. Hub-bard says good-bye to Margaret and makes exit, followed by Chalmers.)

(Margaret remains standing, one hand resting on table, the other hand to her breast. She is thinking, establishing in her mind the connection between Knox and what she has overheard, and in process of reaching the conclusion that Knox is in danger.)

(Tommy, having vainly waited to be discovered, crawls out dispiritedly, and takes Margaret by the hand. She scarcely notices him.)

TOMMY
(Dolefully.) Don't you want to play any more? (Margaret does not reply). I was a good Indian.

MARGARET

(Suddenly becoming aware of herself and breaking down.
She stoops and clasps Tommy in her arms, crying out, in
anxiety and fear, and from love of her boy.) Oh, Tommy!
Tommy!

Curtain

ACT II

SCENE. SITTING ROOM OF HOWARD KNOX— DIMLY LIGHTED. TIME, EIGHT O'CLOCK IN THE EVENING.

Entrance from hallway at side to right. At right rear is locked door leading to a room which dees not belong to Knox's suite. At rear center is fireplace. At left rear door leading to Knox's bedroom. At left are windows facing on street. Near these windows is a large library table littered with books, magazines, government reports, etc. To the right of center, midway forward, is a Hat-top desk. On it is a desk telephone. Behind it, so that one sitting in it faces audience, is revolving desk-chair. Also, on desk, are letters in their envelopes, etc. Against clear wall-spaces are bookcases and filing cabinets. Of special note is bookcase, containing large books, and not more than five feet high, which is against wall between fireplace and door to bedroom.

Curtain discloses empty stage.

(After a slight interval, door at right rear is shaken and agitated. After slight further interval, door is opened inward upon stage. A Man's head appears, cautiously looking around).

(Man enters, turns up lights, is followed by second Man. Both are clad decently, in knock-about business suits and starched collars, cuffs, etc. They are trim, deft, determined men).

(Following upon them, enters Hubbard. He looks about room, crosses to desk, picks up a letter, and reads address).

HUBBARD
This is Knox's room all right

FIRST MAN
Trust us for that.

SECOND MAN
We were lucky the guy with the whiskers moved out of that other room only this afternoon.

FIRST MAN
His key hadn't come down yet when I engaged it.

HUBBARD
Well, get to work. That must be his bedroom.

(He goes to door of bedroom, opens, and peers in, turns on electric lights of bedroom, turns them out, then turns back to men.) You know what it is—a bunch of documents and letters. If we find it there is a clean five hundred each for you, in addition to your regular pay.

(While the conversation goes on, all three engage in a careful search of desk, drawers, filing cabinets, bookcases, etc.)

SECOND MAN
Old Starkweather must want them bad.

HUBBARD
  Sh-h. Don't even breathe his name.

SECOND MAN
  His nibs is damned exclusive, ain't he?

FIRST MAN
  I've never got a direct instruction from him, and I've worked for him longer than you.

SECOND MAN
  Yes, and you worked for him for over two years before you knew who was hiring you.

HUBBARD
  (To First Man.) You'd better go out in the hall and keep a watch for Knox. He may come in any time.

  (First Man produces skeleton keys and goes to door at right. The first key opens it. Leaving door slightly ajar, he makes exit.)

  (Desk telephone rings and startles Hubbard.)

SECOND MAN
  (Grinning at Hubbard's alarm.)

  It's only the phone.

HUBBARD
  (Proceeding with search.) I suppose you've done lots of work for Stark—

SECOND MAN
  (Mimicking him.) Sh-h. Don't breathe his name.

(Telephone rings again and again, insistently, urgently.)

HUBBARD
(Disguising his voice.) Hello—Yes.

(Shows surprise, seems to recognize the voice, and smiles knowingly.)

No, this is not Knox. Some mistake. Wrong number—

(Hanging up receiver and speaking to Second Man in natural voice.) She did hang up quick.

SECOND MAN
You seemed to recognize her.

HUBBARD
No, I only thought I did.

(A pause, while they search.)

SECOND MAN
I've never spoken a word to his nibs in my life. And I've drawn his pay for years too.

HUBBARD
What of it?

SECOND MAN
(Complainingly.) He don't know I exist.

HUBBARD
(Pulling open a desk drawer and examining contents.)

The pay's all right, isn't it?

SECOND MAN

It sure is, but I guess I earn every cent of it. (First Man enters through door at right He moves hurriedly but cautiously. Shuts door behind him, but neglects to re-lock it.)

FIRST MAN

Somebody just left the elevator and is coming down the hall.

(Hubbard, First Man, and Second Man, all start for door at right rear.)

(First Man pauses and looks around to see if room is in order. Sees desk-drawer which Hubbard has neglected to close, goes back and closes it.)

(Hubbard and Second Man make exit.)

(First Man turns lights low and makes exit.)

(Sound of locking door is heard.)

(A pause.)

(A knocking at door to right. A pause. Then door opens and Gilford enters. He turns up lights, strolls about room, looks at watch, and sits down in chair near right of fireplace.) (Sound of key in lock of door to right.) (Door opens, and Knox enters, key in hand. Sees Gifford.)

KNOX

(Advancing to meet him at fireplace and shaking hands.) How did you get in?

GIFFORD

I let myself in. The door was unlocked.

KNOX

I must have forgotten it.

GIFFORD

(Drawing bundle of documents from inside breast pocket and handing them to Knox.) Well, there they are.

KNOX

(Fingering them curiously.) You are sure they are originals? (Gifford nods.)

I can't take any chances, you know. If Gherst changed his mind after I gave my speech and refused to show the originals—such things have happened.

GIFFORD

That's what I told him. He was firm on giving duplicates, and for awhile it looked as if my trip to New York was wasted. But I stuck to my guns. It was originals or nothing with you, I said, and he finally gave in.

KNOX

(Holding up documents.) I can't tell you what they mean to me, nor how grateful—

GIFFORD

(Interrupting.) That's all right. Don't mention it. Gherst is wild for the chance. It will do organized labor a heap of good. And you are able to say your own say at the same time. How's that compensation act coming on?

KNOX

(Wearily.) The same old story. It will never come before the House. It is dying in committee. What can you expect of the Committee of Judiciary?—composed as it is of ex-railroad judges and ex-railroad lawyers.

GIFFORD

The railroad brotherhoods are keen on getting that bill
through.

KNOX

Well, they won't, and they never will until they learn to
vote right. When will your labor leaders quit the strike and
boycott and lead your men to political action?

GIFFORD

(Holding out hand.) Well, so long. I've got to trot, and I
haven't time to tell you why I think political action would
destroy the trade union movement.

(Knox tosses documents on top of low bookcase between
fireplace and bedroom door, and starts to shake hands.)
You're damn careless with those papers. You wouldn't be if
you knew how much Gherst paid for them.

GIFFORD

You don't appreciate that other crowd. It stops at nothing.

KNOX

I won't take my eyes off of them. And I'll take them to bed
with me to-night for safety. Besides, there is no danger.
Nobody but you knows I have them.

GIFFORD

(Proceeding toward door to right.) I'd hate to be in
Starkweather's office when he discovers what's happened.
There'll be some bad half hours for somebody. (Pausing at
door.) Give them hell to-morrow, good and plenty. I'm going

to be in a gallery. So long. (Makes exit.)

(Knox crosses to windows, which he opens, returns to desk, seats himself in revolving chair, and begins opening his correspondence.) (A knock at door to right.)

KNOX

Come in.

(Hubbard enters, advances to desk, but does not shake hands. They greet each other, and Hubbard sits down in chair to left of desk.) (Knox, still holding an open letter, re-volves chair so as to face his visitor. He waits for Hubbabd to speak.)

HUBBARD

There is no use beating about the bush with a man like you. I know that. You are direct, and so am I. You know my position well enough to be assured that I am empowered to treat with you.

KNOX

Oh, yes; I know.

HUBBARD

What we want is to have you friendly.

KNOX

That is easy enough. When the Interests become upright and honest—

HUBBARD

Save that for your speech. We are talking privately. We can make it well worth your while—

KNOX

(Angrily.) If you think you can bribe me—

HUBBARD

(Suavely.) Not at all. Not the slightest suspicion of it. The point is this. You are a congressman. A congressman's career depends on his membership in good committees. At the present you are buried in the dead Committee on Coinage, Weights, and Measures. If you say the word you can be appointed to the livest committee—

KNOX

(Interrupting.) You have these appointments to give?

HUBBARD

Surely. Else why should I be here? It can be managed.

KNOX

(Meditatively.) I thought our government was rotten enough, but I never dreamed that House appointments were hawked around by the Interests in this fashion.

HUBBARD

You have not given your answer.

KNOX

You should have known my answer in advance.

HUBBARD

There is an alternative. You are interested in social problems. You are a student of sociology. Those whom I represent are genuinely interested in you. We are prepared, so that you may pursue your researches more deeply—we are prepared to send you to Europe. There, in that vast sociological laboratory, far from the jangling strife of politics, you will have every opportunity to study. We are prepared to send you for a period of ten years. You will receive ten thousand dollars a year, and, in addition, the day your steamer leaves New York, you will receive a lump sum of one hundred thousand dollars.

KNOX

And this is the way men are bought

HUBBARD

It is purely an educational matter.

KNOX

Now it is you who are beating about the bush.

HUBBARD

(Decisively.) Very well then. What price do you set on yourself?

KNOX

You want me to quit—to leave politics, everything? You want to buy my soul?

HUBBARD

More than that. We want to buy those documents and letters.

KNOX

(Showing a slight start.) What documents and letters?

HUBBARD

You are beating around the bush in turn. There is no need for an honest man to lie even—

KNOX

(Interrupting.) To you.

HUBBARD

(Smiling.) Even to me. I watched you closely when I mentioned the letters. You gave yourself away. You knew I meant the letters stolen by Gherst from Starkweather's private files—the letters you intended using to-morrow.

KNOX

Intend using to-morrow.

HUBBARD

Precisely. It is the same thing. What is the price? Set it.

KNOX

I have nothing to sell. I am not on the market.

HUBBARD

One moment. Don't make up your mind hastily. You don't know with whom you have to deal. Those letters will not appear in your speech to-morrow. Take that from me. It would be far wiser to sell for a fortune than to get nothing for them and at the same time not use them.

(A knock at door to right startles Hubbard.)

KNOX

(Intending to say, "Come in") Come—

HUBBARD

(Interrupting.) Hush. Don't. I cannot be seen here.

KNOX

(Laughing.) You fear the contamination of my company. (The knock is repeated.)

HUBBARD

(In alarm, rising, as Knox purses his lips to bid them enter.) Don't let anybody in. I don't want to be seen here—with you. Besides, my presence will not put you in a good light.

KNOX

(Also rising, starting toward door.) What I do is always open to the world. I see no one whom I should not permit the world to know I saw.

(Knox starts toward door to open it.) (Hubbabd, looking about him in alarm, flees across stage and into bedroom, closing the door. During all the following scene, Hubbard, from time to time, opens door, and peers out at what is going on.)

KNOX

(Opening door, and recoiling.) Margaret! Mrs. Chalmers!

(Margaret enters, followed by Tommy and Linda. Margaret is in evening dress covered by evening cloak.)

MARGARET

(Shaking hands with Knox.) Forgive me, but I had to see you. I could not get you on the telephone. I called and called, and the best I could do was to get the wrong number.

KNOX

(Recovering from his astonishment.) Yes. I am glad.

(Seeing Tommy.) Hello, Tommy.

(Knox holds out his hand, and Tommy shakes it gravely. Linda stays in back-ground. Her face is troubled.)

TOMMY

How do you do?

MARGARET

There was no other way, and it was so necessary for me to warn you. I brought Tommy and Linda along to chaperon me.

(She looks curiously around room, specially indicating filing cabinets and the stacks of government reports on table.) Your laboratory.

KNOX

Ah, if I were only as great a sociological wizard as Edison is a wizard in physical sciences.

MARGARET

But you are. You labor more mightily than you admit—or dare to think. Oh, I know you—better than you do yourself.

TOMMY

Do you read all those books?

KNOX

Yes, I am still going to school and studying hard. What are you going to study to be when you grow up?

(Tommy meditates but does not answer.)

President of these great United States?

TOMMY

(Shaking his head.) Father says the President doesn't amount
to much.

KNOX

Not a Lincoln?

(Tommy is in doubt.)

MARGARET

But don't you remember what a great good man Lincoln was?
You remember I told you?

TOMMY

(Shaking his head slowly.) But I don't want to be killed.—I'll
tell you what!

KNOX

What?

TOMMY

I want to be a senator like father. He makes them dance.

(Margaret is shocked, and Knox's eyes twinkle.)

KNOX

Makes whom dance?

TOMMY

(Puzzled.) I don't know.

(With added confidence.) But he makes them dance just the
same.

(Margaret makes a signal to Linda to take Tommy across the room.)

LINDA

(Starting to cross stage to left.) Come, Tommy. Let us look out of the window.

TOMMY

I'd rather talk with Mr. Knox.

MARGARET

Please do, Tommy. Mamma wants to talk to Mr. Knox.

(Tommy yields, and crosses to right, where he joins Linda in looking out of the window.)

MARGARET

You might ask me to take a seat

KNOX

Oh! I beg pardon.

(He draws up a comfortable chair for her, and seats himself in desk-chair, facing her.)

MARGARET

I have only a few minutes. Tom is at father's, and I am to pick him up there and go on to that dinner, after I've taken Tommy home.

KNOX

But your maid?

MARGARET

Linda? Wild horses could not drag from her anything that she thought would harm me. So intense is her fidelity that it almost shames me. I do not deserve it. But this is not what I came to you about.

(She speaks the following hurriedly.) After you left this afternoon, something happened. Father received a telegram. It seemed most important. His secretary followed upon the heels of the telegram. Father called Tom and Mr. Hubbard to him and they held a conference. I think they have discovered the loss of the documents, and that they believe you have them. I did not hear them mention your name, yet I am absolutely certain that they were talking about you. Also, I could tell from father's face that something was terribly wrong. Oh, be careful! Do be careful!

KNOX

There is no danger, I assure you.

MARGARET

But you do not know them. I tell you you do not know them. They will stop at nothing—at nothing. Father believes he is right in all that he does.

KNOX

I know. That is what makes him so formidable. He has an ethical sanction.

MARGARET

(Nodding.) It is his religion.

KNOX

And, like any religion with a narrow-minded man, it runs to mania.

MARGARET

He believes that civilization rests on him, and that it is his sacred duty to preserve civilization.

KNOX

I know. I know.

MARGARET

But you? But you? You are in danger.

KNOX

No; I shall remain in to-night. To-morrow, in the broad light of midday, I shall proceed to the House and give my speech.

MARGARET

(Wildly.) Oh, if anything should happen to you!

KNOX

(Looking at her searchingly.) You do care?

(Margaret nods, with eyes suddenly downcast.) For Howard Knox, the reformer? Or for me, the man?

MARGARET

(Impulsively.) Oh, why must a woman forever remain quiet? Why should I not tell you what you already know?—what you must already know? I do care for you—for man and reformer, both—for—

(She is aflame, but abruptly ceases and glances across at Tommy by the window, warned instinctively that she must not give way to love in her child's presence.)

Linda! Will you take Tommy down to the machine—

KNOX

(Alarmed, interrupting, in low voice.) What are you doing?

MARGARET

(Hushing Knox with a gesture.) I'll follow you right down.

(Linda and Tommy proceed across stage toward right exit.)

TOMMY

(Pausing before Knox and gravely extending his hand.) Good evening, Mr. Knox.

KNOX

(Awkwardly.) Good evening, Tommy. You take my word for it, and look up this Lincoln question.

TOMMY

I shall. I'll ask father about it.

MARGARET

(Significantly.) You attend to that, Linda. Nobody must know—this.

(Linda nods.)

(Linda and Tommy make exit to right.)

(Margaret, seated, slips back her cloak, revealing herself in evening gown, and looks at Knox sumptuously, lovingly, and willingly.)

KNOX

(Inflamed by the sight of her.) Don't! Don't! I can't stand it. Such sight of you fills me with madness.

(Margaret laughs low and triumphantly.) I don't want to think of you as a woman. I must not. Allow me.

(He rises and attempts to draw cloak about her shoulders, but she resists him. Yet does he succeed in partly cloaking her.)

MARGARET

I want you to see me as a woman. I want you to think of me as a woman. I want you mad for me.

(She holds out her arms, the cloak slipping from them.)

I want—don't you see what I want?——

(Knox sinks back in chair, attempting to shield his eyes with his hand.)

(Slipping cloak fully back from her again.)

Look at me.

KNOX

(Looking, coming to his feet, and approaching her, with extended arms, murmuring softly.) Margaret. Margaret.

(Margaret rises to meet him, and they are clasped in each other's arms.)

(Hubbard, peering forth through door, looks at them with an expression of cynical amusement. His gaze wan-ders, and he sees the documents, within arm's reach, on top of bookcase. He picks up documents, holds them to the light of stage to glance at them, and, with triumphant expression on face, disappears and closes door.)

KNOX

(Holding Margaret from him and looking at her.) I love you. I do love you. But I had resolved never to speak it, never to let you know.

MARGARET

Silly man. I have known long that you loved me. You have told me so often and in so many ways. You could not look at me without telling me.

KNOX

You saw?

MARGARET

How could I help seeing? I was a woman. Only, with your voice you never spoke a word. Sit down, there, where I may look at you, and let me tell you. I shall do the speaking now.

(She urges him back into the desk-chair, and reseats herself.) (She makes as if to pull the cloak around 'her.) Shall I?

KNOX

(Vehemently.) No, no! As you are. Let me feast my eyes upon you who are mine. I must be dreaming.

MARGARET

(With a low, satisfied laugh of triumph.) Oh, you men! As of old, and as forever, you must be wooed through your senses. Did I display the wisdom of an Hypatia, the science of a Madam Curie, yet would you keep your iron control, throttling the voice of your heart with silence. But let me for a moment be Lilith, for a moment lay aside this garment constructed for the purpose of keeping out the chill of night, and on the instant you are fire and aflame, all voluble with love's desire.

KNOX

(Protestingly.) Margaret! It is not fair!

MARGARET

I love you—and—you?

KNOX

(Fervently and reverently.) I love you.

MARGARET

Then listen. I have told you of my girlhood and my dreams.
I wanted to do what you are so nobly doing. And I did
nothing. I could do nothing. I was not permitted. Always
was I compelled to hold myself in check. It was to do what
you are doing, that I married. And that, too, failed me.
My husband became a henchman of the Interests, my own
father's tool for the perpetuation of the evils against which I
desired to fight.

(She pauses.) It has been a long fight, and I have been very
tired, for always did I confront failure. My husband—I did
not love him. I never loved him. I sold myself for the Cause,
and the cause profited nothing. (Pause.) Often, I have lost
faith—faith in everything, in God and man, in the hope of
any righteousness ever prevailing. But again and again, by
what you are doing, have you awakened me. I came to-night
with no thought of self. I came to warn you, to help the good
work on. I remained—thank God!—I remained to love you—
and to be loved by you. I suddenly found myself, looking at
you, very weary. I wanted you—you, more than anything in
the world.

(She holds out her arms.) Come to me. I want you—now.

(Knox, in an ecstacy, comes to her. He seats himself on the
broad arm of the chair and is drawn into her arms.)

KNOX

But I have been tired at times. I was very tired to-night—and you came. And now I am glad, only glad.

MARGARET

I have been wanton to-night. I confess it. I am proud of it. But it was not—professional. It was the first time in my life. Almost do I regret—almost do I regret that I did not do it sooner—it has been crowned with such success. You have held me in your arms—your arms. Oh, you will never know what that first embrace meant to me. I am not a clod. I am not iron nor stone. I am a woman—a warm, breathing woman—.

(She rises, and draws him to his feet.)

Kiss me, my dear lord and lover. Kiss me. (They embrace.)

KNOX

(Passionately, looking about him wildly as if in search of something.) What shall we do?

(Suddenly releasing her and sinking back in his own chair almost in collapse.) No. It cannot be. It is impossible. Oh, why could we not have met long ago? We would have worked together. What a comradeship it would have been.

MARGARET

But it is not too late.

KNOX

I have no right to you.

MARGARET

(Misunderstanding.) My husband? He has not been my husband for years. He has no rights. Who, but you whom I love, has any rights?

KNOX

No; it is not that.

(Snapping his fingers.) That for him.

(Breaking down.) Oh, if I were only the man, and not the reformer! If I had no work to do!

MARGARET

(Coming to the back of his chair and caressing his hair.) We can work together.

KNOX

(Shaking his head under her fingers.) Don't! Don't!

(She persists, and lays her cheek against his.) You make it so hard. You tempt me so.

(He rises suddenly, takes her two hands in his, leads her gently to her chair, seats her, and reseats himself in desk-chair.) Listen. It is not your husband. But I have no right to you. Nor have you a right to me.

MARGARET

(Interrupting, jealously.) And who but I has any right to you?

KNOX

(Smiling sadly.) No; it is not that. There is no other woman. You are the one woman for me. But there are many others who have greater rights in me than you. I have been chosen by two hundred thousand citizens to represent them in the

Congress of the United States. And there are many more—

(He breaks off suddenly and looks at her, at her arms and shoulders.) Yes, please. Cover them up. Help me not to forget.

(Margaret does not obey.) There are many more who have rights in me—the people, all the people, whose cause I have made mine. The children—there are two million child laborers in these United States. I cannot betray them. I cannot steal my happiness from them. This afternoon I talked of theft. But would not this, too, be theft?

MARGARET

(Sharply.) Howard! Wake up! Has our happiness turned your head?

KNOX

(Sadly.) Almost—and for a few wild moments, quite. There are all the children. Did I ever tell you of the tenement child, who when asked how he knew when spring came, answered: When he saw the saloons put up their swing doors.

MARGARET

(Irritated.) But what has all that to do with one man and one woman loving?

KNOX

Suppose we loved—you and I; suppose we loosed all the reins of our love. What would happen? You remember Gorki, the Russian patriot, when he came to New York, aflame with passion for the Russian revolution. His purpose in visiting the land of liberty was to raise funds for that revolution. And because his marriage to the woman he loved was not of the essentially legal sort worshiped by the shopkeepers, and because the newspapers made a sensation of it, his whole mission was brought to failure. He was laughed and derided out of the esteem of the American people. That is what would happen to me. I should be slandered and laughed at. My power would be gone.

MARGARET

And even if so—what of it? Be slandered and laughed at. We will have each other. Other men will rise up to lead the people, and leading the people is a thankless task. Life is so short. We must clutch for the morsel of happiness that may be ours.

KNOX

Ah, if you knew, as I look into your eyes, how easy it would be to throw everything to the winds. But it would be theft.

MARGARET

(Rebelliously.) Let it be theft. Life is so short, dear. We are the biggest facts in the world—to each other.

KNOX

It is not myself alone, nor all my people. A moment ago you said no one but I had any right to you. You were wrong. Your child—

MARGARET

(In sudden pain, pleadingly.) Don't!

KNOX

I must. I must save myself—and you. Tommy has rights in you. Theft again. What other name for it if you steal your happiness from him?

MARGARET

(Bending her head forward on her hand and weeping.) I have been so lonely—and then you—you came, and the world grew bright and warm—a few short minutes ago you held me—in your arms—a few short minutes ago and it seemed my dream of happiness had come true—and now you dash it from me—

KNOX

(Struggling to control himself now that she is no longer looking at him.) No; I ask you to dash it from yourself. I am not too strong. You must help me. You must call your child to your aid in helping me. I could go mad for you now—

(Rising impulsively and coming to her with arms outstretched to clasp her.) Right now—

MARGARET

(Abruptly raising her head, and with one outstretched arm preventing the embrace.) Wait.

(She bows her head on her hand for a moment, to think and to win control of herself.)

(Lifting her head and looking at him.) Sit down—please.

(Knox reseats himself.)

(A pause, during which she looks at him and loves him.) Dear, I do so love you—

(Knox loses control and starts to rise.) No! Sit there. I was weak. Yet I am not sorry. You are right. We must forego each other. We cannot be thieves, even for love's sake. Yet I am glad that this has happened—that I have lain in your arms and had your lips on mine. The memory of it will be sweet always.

(She draws her cloak around her, and rises.)

(Knox rises.) You are right. The future belongs to the children. There lies duty—yours, and mine in my small way. I am going now. We must not see each other ever again. We must work—and forget. But remember, my heart goes with you into the fight. My prayers will accompany every stroke.

(She hesitates, pauses, draws her cloak thoroughly around her in evidence of departure.) Dear—will you kiss me— once—one last time? (There is no passion in this kiss, which is the kiss of renunciation. Margaret herself terminates the embrace.)

(Knox accompanies her silently to the door and places hand on knob.) I wish I had something of you to have with me always—a photograph, that little one, you remember, which I liked so. (She nods.) Don't run the risk of sending it by messenger. Just mail it ordinarily.

MARGARET

I shall mail it to-morrow. I'll drop it in the box myself.

KNOX

(Kissing her hand.) Good-bye.

MARGARET

(lingeringly.) But oh, my dear, I am glad and proud for what has happened. I would not erase a single line of it.

(She indicates for Knox to open door, which he does, but which he immediately closes as she continues speaking.) There must be immortality. There must be a future life where you and I shall meet again. Good-bye.

(They press each other's hands.)

(Exit Margaret.)

(Knox stands a moment, staring at closed door, turns and looks about him indecisively, sees chair in which Margaret sat, goes over to it, kneels down, and buries his face.)

(Door to bedroom opens slowly and Hubbard peers out cautiously. He cannot see Knox.)

HUBBARD

(Advancing, surprised.) What the deuce? Everybody gone?

KNOX

(Startled to his feet.) Where the devil did you come from?

HUBBARD

(Indicating bedroom.) In there. I was in there all the time.

KNOX

(Endeavoring to pass it off.) Oh, I had forgotten about you. Well, my callers are gone.

HUBBARD

(Walking over close to him and laughing at him with affected amusement.) Honest men are such dubs when they do go wrong.

KNOX

The door was closed all the time. You would not have dared to spy upon me.

HUBBARD

There was something familiar about the lady's voice.

KNOX

You heard!—what did you hear?

HUBBARD

Oh, nothing, nothing—a murmur of voices—and the woman's—I could swear I have heard her voice before.

(Knox shows his relief.) Well, so long.

(Starts to move toward exit to right.) You won't reconsider your decision?

KNOX

(Shaking his head.)

HUBBARD

(Pausing, open door in hand, and laughing cynically.) And yet it was but a moment ago that it seemed I heard you say there was no one whom you would not permit the world to know you saw.

(Starting.) What do you mean?

HUBBARD

Good-bye.

(Hubbard makes exit and closes door.) (Knox wanders aimlessly to his desk, glances at the letter he was reading of which had been interrupted by Hubbard's entry of first act, suddenly recollects the package of documents, and walks to low bookcase and looks on top.)

KNOX

(Stunned.) The thief!

(He looks about him wildly, then rushes like a madman in pursuit of Hubbard, making exit to right and leaving the door Hying open.) (Empty stage for a moment.)

Curtain

ACT III

SCENE.

The library, used as a sort of semi-office by Starkweather at such times when he is in Washington. Door to right; also, door to right rear. At left rear is an alcove, without hangings, which is dark. To left are windows. To left, near windows, a fiat-top desk, with desk-chair and desk-telephone. Also, on desk, conspicuously, is a heavy dispatch box. At the center rear is a large screen. Extending across center back of room are heavy, old-fashioned bookcases, with swinging glass doors. The bookcases narrow about four feet from the floor, thus forming a ledge. Between left end of bookcases and alcove at left rear, high up on wall, hangs a large painting or steel engraving of Abraham Lincoln. In design and furnishings, it is a simple chaste room, coldly rigid and slightly old-fashioned.

It is 9:30 in the morning of the day succeeding previous act.

Curtain discloses Starkweather seated at desk, and Dobleman, to right of desk, standing.

STARKWEATHER

All right, though it is an unimportant publication. I'll subscribe.

DOBLEMAN

(Making note on pad.) Very well, sir. Two thousand.

(He consults his notes.) Then there is Vanderwater's Magazine. Your subscription is due.

STARKWEATHER

How much?

DOBLEMAN

You have been paying fifteen thousand.

STARKWEATHER

It is too much. What is the regular subscription?

DOBLEMAN

A dollar a year.

STARKWEATHER

(Shaking his head emphatically.) It is too much.

DOBLEMAN

Professor Vanderwater also does good work with his lecturing. He is regularly on the Chautauqua Courses, and at that big meeting of the National Civic Federation, his speech was exceptionally telling.

STARKWEATHER

(Doubtfully, about to give in.) All right—

(He pauses, as if recollecting something.) (Dobleman has begun to write down the note.) No. I remember there was something in the papers about this Professor Vanderwater—a divorce, wasn't it? He has impaired his authority and his usefulness to me.

DOBLEMAN

It was his wife's fault.

STARKWEATHER

It is immaterial. His usefulness is impaired. Cut him down to
ten thousand. It will teach him a lesson.

DOBLEMAN

Very good, sir.

STARKWEATHER

And the customary twenty thousand to Cartwrights.

DOBLEMAN

(Hesitatingly.) They have asked for more. They have enlarged
the magazine, reorganized the stock, staff, everything.

STARKWEATHER

Hubbard's writing for it, isn't he?

DOBLEMAN

Yes, sir. And though I don't know, it is whispered that he is
one of the heavy stockholders.

STARKWEATHER

A very capable man. He has served me well. How much do
they want?

DOBLEMAN

They say that Nettman series of articles cost them twelve
thousand alone, and that they believe, in view of the

exceptional service they are prepared to render, and are rendering, fifty thousand—

STARKWEATHER

(Shortly.) All right. How much have I given to University of Hanover this year?

DOBLEMAN

Seven—nine millions, including that new library.

STARKWEATHER

(Sighing.) Education does cost. Anything more this morning?

DOBLEMAN

(Consulting notes.) Just one other—Mr. Rutland. His church, you know, sir, and that theological college. He told me he had been talking it over with you. He is anxious to know.

STARKWEATHER

He's very keen, I must say. Fifty thousand for the church, and a hundred thousand for the college—I ask you, candidly, is he worth it?

DOBLEMAN

The church is a very powerful molder of public opinion, and Mr. Rutland is very impressive. (Running over the notes and producing a clipping.) This is what he said in his sermon two weeks ago: "God has given to Mr. Starkweather the talent for making money as truly as God has given to other men the genius which manifests itself in literature and the arts and sciences."

STARKWEATHER

(Pleased.) He says it well.

DOBLEMAN

(Producing another clipping.) And this he said about you in last Sunday's sermon: "We are to-day rejoicing in the great light of the consecration of a great wealth to the advancement of the race. This vast wealth has been so consecrated by a man who all through life has walked in accord with the word, The love of Christ constraineth me.'"

STARKWEATHER

(Meditatively.) Dobleman, I have meant well. I mean well. I shall always mean well. I believe I am one of those few men, to whom God, in his infinite wisdom, has given the stewardship of the people's wealth. It is a high trust, and despite the abuse and vilification heaped upon me, I shall remain faithful to it.

(Changing his tone abruptly to businesslike briskness.) Very well. See that Mr. Rutland gets what he has asked for.

DOBLEMAN

Very good, sir. I shall telephone him. I know he is anxious to hear.

(Starting to leave the room.) Shall I make the checks out in the usual way?

STARKWEATHER

Yes: except the Rutland one. I'll sign that myself. Let the others go through the regular channels. We take the 2:10 train for New York. Are you ready?

DOBLEMAN
(Indicating dispatch box.) All, except the dispatch box.

STARKWEATHER
I'll take care of that myself.

(Dobleman starts to make exit to left, and Starkweather, taking notebook from pocket, glances into it, and looks up.)

Dobleman.

DOBLEMAN
(Pausing.) Yes, sir.

STARKWEATHER
Mrs. Chalmers is here, isn't she?

DOBLEMAN
Yes, sir. She came a few minutes ago, with her little boy. They are with Mrs. Starkweather.

STARKWEATHER
Please tell Mrs. Chalmers I wish to see her.

DOBLEMAN
Yes, sir.

(Dobleman makes exit.) (Maidservant enters from right rear, with card tray.)

STARKWEATHER
(Examining card.) Show him in.

(Maidservant makes exit right rear). (Pause, during which Starkweather consults notebook.) (Maidservant re-enters, showing in Hubbard.)

(Hubbard advances to desk.) (Starkweather is so glad to see him that he half rises from his chair to shake hands.)

STARKWEATHER

(Heartily.) I can only tell you that what you did was wonderful. Your telephone last night was a great relief. Where are they?

HUBBARD

(Drawing package of documents from inside breast pocket and handing them over.) There they are—the complete set. I was fortunate.

STARKWEATHER

(Opening package and glancing at a number of the documents while he talks.) You are modest, Mr. Hubbard.— It required more—than fortune.—It required ability—of no mean order.—The time was short.—You had to think and act—with too great immediacy to be merely fortunate.

(Hubbard bows, while Starkweather rearranges package.)

There is no need for me to tell you how I appreciate your service. I have increased my subscription to Cartwright's to fifty thousand, and I shall speak to Dobleman, who will remit to you a more substantial acknowledgment than my mere thanks for the inestimable service you have rendered.

(Hubbard bows.)

You—ah—you have read the documents?

HUBBARD

I glanced through them. They were indeed serious. But we have spiked Knox's guns. Without them, that speech of his this afternoon becomes a farce—a howling farce. Be sure you take good care of them.

(Indicating documents, which Starkweather still holds.) Gherst has a long arm.

STARKWEATHER

He cannot reach me here. Besides, I go to New York to-day, and I shall carry them with me. Mr. Hubbard, you will forgive me—

(Starting to pack dispatch box with papers and letters lying on desk.) I am very busy.

HUBBARD

(Taking the hint.) Yes, I understand. I shall be going now. I have to be at the Club in five minutes.

STARKWEATHER

(In course of packing dispatch box, he sets certain packets of papers and several medium-sized account books to one side in an orderly pile. He talks while he packs, and Hubbard waits.) I should like to talk with you some more— in New York. Next time you are in town be sure to see me. I am thinking of buying the Parthenon Magazine, and of changing its policy. I should like to have you negotiate this, and there are other important things as well. Good day, Mr. Hubbard. I shall see you in New York—soon.

(Hubbard and Starkweather shake hands.)

(Hubbard starts to make exit to right rear.)

(Margaret enters from right rear.)

(Starkweather goes on packing dispatch box through following scene.)

HUBBARD

Mrs. Chalmers.

(Holding out hand, which Margaret takes very coldly, scarcely inclining her head, and starting to pass on.) (Speaking suddenly and savagely.) You needn't be so high and lofty, Mrs. Chalmers.

MARGARET

(Pausing and looking at him curiously as if to ascertain whether he has been drinking.) I do not understand.

HUBBARD

You always treated me this way, but the time for it is past. I won't stand for your superior goodness any more. You really impressed me with it for a long time, and you made me walk small. But I know better now. A pretty game you've been playing—you, who are like any other woman. Well, you know where you were last night. So do I.

MARGARET

You are impudent.

HUBBARD

(Doggedly.) I said I knew where you were last night. Mr. Knox also knows where you were. But I'll wager your husband doesn't.

MARGARET

You spy!

(Indicating her father.) I suppose you have told—him.

HUBBARD
  Why should I?

MARGARET
  You are his creature.

HUBBARD
  If it will ease your suspense, let me tell you that I have not
  told him. But I do protest to you that you must treat me with
  more—more kindness.

  (Margaret makes no sign but passes on utterly oblivious
  of him.) (Hubbard stares angrily at her and makes exit)
  (Starkweather, who is finishing packing, puts the documents
  last inside box, and closes and locks it. To one side is the
  orderly stack of the several account books and packets of
  papers.)

STARKWEATHER
  Good morning, Margaret. I sent for you because we did not
  finish that talk last night. Sit down.

  (She gets a chair for herself and sits down.)

  You always were hard to manage, Margaret. You have had
  too much will for a woman. Yet I did my best for you. Your
  marriage with Tom was especially auspicious—a rising man,
  of good family and a gentleman, eminently suitable—

MARGARET
  (Interrupting bitterly.) I don't think you were considering
  your daughter at all in the matter. I know your views
  on woman and woman's place. I have never counted for
  anything with you. Neither has mother, nor Connie, when
  business was uppermost, and business always is uppermost
  with you. I sometimes wonder if you think a woman has

114

a soul. As for my marriage—you saw that Tom could be useful to you. He had the various distinctive points you have mentioned. Better than that he was pliable, capable of being molded to perform your work, to manipulate machine politics and procure for you the legislation you desired. You did not consider what kind of a husband he would make for your daughter whom you did not know. But you gave your daughter to him—sold her to him—because you needed him—

(Laughs hysterically.) In your business.

STARKWEATHER

(Angrily.) Margaret! You must not speak that way. (Relaxing.)

Ah, you do not change. You were always that way, always bent on having your will—

MARGARET

Would to God I had been more successful in having it.

STARKWEATHER

(Testily.) This is all beside the question. I sent for you to tell you that this must stop—this association with a man of the type and character of Knox—a dreamer, a charlatan, a scoundrel—

MARGARET

It is not necessary to abuse him.

STARKWEATHER

It must stop—that is all. Do you understand? It must stop.

MARGARET

(Quietly.) It has stopped. I doubt that I shall ever see him again. He will never come to my house again, at any rate. Are you satisfied?

STARKWEATHER

Perfectly. Of course, you know I have never doubted you—that—that way.

MARGARET

(Quietly.) How little you know women. In your comprehension we are automatons, puppets, with no hearts nor heats of desire of our own, with no springs of conduct save those of the immaculate and puritanical sort that New England crystallized a century or so ago.

STARKWEATHER

(Suspiciously.) You mean that you and this man—?

MARGARET

I mean nothing has passed between us. I mean that I am Tom's wife and Tommy's mother. What I did mean, you have no more understood than you understand me—or any woman.

STARKWEATHER

(Relieved.) It is well.

MARGARET

(Continuing.) And it is so easy. The concept is simple. A woman is human. That is all. Yet I do believe it is news to you.

(Enters Dobleman from right carrying a check in his hand. Starkweather, about to speak, pauses.) (Dobleman hesitates, and Starkweather nods for him to advance.)

DOBLEMAN

(Greeting Margaret, and addressing Starkweather.) This check. You said you would sign it yourself.

STARKWEATHER

Yes, that is Rutland's. (Looks for pen.)

(Dobleman offers his fountain pen.) No; my own pen.

(Unlocks dispatch box, gets pen, and signs check. Leaves dispatch box open.) (Dobleman takes check and makes exit to right.)

STARKWEATHER

(Picking up documents from top of pile in open box.)

This man Knox. I studied him yesterday. A man of great energy and ideals. Unfortunately, he is a sentimentalist. He means right—I grant him that. But he does not understand practical conditions. He is more dangerous to the welfare of the United States than ten thousand anarchists. And he is not practical. (Holding up documents.)

Behold, stolen from my private files by a yellow journal sneak thief and turned over to him. He thought to buttress his speech with them this afternoon. And yet, so hopelessly unpractical is he, that you see they are already back in the rightful owner's hands.

MARGARET

Then his speech is ruined?

117

STARKWEATHER

Absolutely. The wheels are all ready to turn. The good people of the United States will dismiss him with roars of laughter—a good phrase, that: Hubbard's, I believe.

(Dropping documents on the open cover of dispatch box, picking up the pile of several account books and packets of papers, and rising.) One moment. I must put these away.

(Starkweather goes to alcove at left rear. He presses a button and alcove is lighted by electricity, discovering the face of a large safe. During the following scene he does not look around, being occupied with working the combination, opening the safe, putting away account books and packets of papers, and with examining other packets which are in safe.)

(Margaret looks at documents lying on open cover of dispatch box and glancing quickly about room, takes a sudden resolution. She seizes documents, makes as if to run wildly from the room, stops abruptly to reconsider, and changes her mind. She looks about room for a hiding place, and her eyes rest on portrait of Lincoln. Moving swiftly, picking up a light chair on the way, she goes to corner of bookcase nearest to portrait, steps on chair, and from chair to ledge of bookcase where, clinging, she reaches out and up and drops documents behind portrait. Stepping quickly down, with handkerchief she wipes ledge on which she has stood, also the seat of the chair. She carries chair back to where she found it, and reseats herself in chair by desk.)
(Starkweather locks safe, emerges from alcove, turns off alcove lights, advances to desk chair, and sits down. He is about to close and lock dispatch box when he discovers documents are missing. He is very quiet about it, and examines contents of box care-fully.)

STARKWEATHER

(Quietly.) Has anybody been in the room?

MARGARET

No.

STARKWEATHER

(Looking at her searchingly.) A most unprecedented thing has occurred. When I went to the safe a moment ago, I left these documents on the cover of the dispatch box. Nobody has been in the room but you. The documents are gone. Give them to me.

MARGARET

I have not been out of the room.

STARKWEATHER

I know that. Give them to me.

(A pause.) You have them. Give them to me

MARGARET

I haven't them.

STARKWEATHER

That is a lie. Give them to me.

MARGARET

(Rising.) I tell you I haven't them—

STARKWEATHER

(Also rising.) That is a lie.

MARGARET

(Turning and starting to cross room.) Very well, if you do not believe me—

STARKWEATHER

(Interrupting.) Where are you going?

MARGARET

Home.

STARKWEATHER

(Imperatively.) No, you are not. Come back here.

(Margaret comes back and stands by chair.) You shall not leave this room. Sit down.

MARGARET

I prefer to stand.

STARKWEATHER

Sit down.

(She still stands, and he grips her by arm, forcing her down into chair.) Sit down. Before you leave this room you shall return those documents. This is more important than you realize. It transcends all ordinary things of life as you have known it, and you will compel me to do things far harsher than you can possibly imagine. I can forget that you are a daughter of mine. I can forget that you are even a woman. If I have to tear them from you, I shall get them. Give them to me.

(A pause.) What are you going to do?

(Margaret shrugs her shoulders.) What have you to say?

(Margaret again shrugs her shoulders.) What have you to say?

MARGARET

Nothing.

STARKWEATHER

(Puzzled, changing tactics, sitting down, and talking calmly.) Let us talk this over quietly. You have no shred of right of any sort to those documents. They are mine. They were stolen by a sneak thief from my private files. Only this morning—a few minutes ago—did I get them back. They are mine, I tell you. They belong to me. Give them back.

MARGARET

I tell you I haven't them.

STARKWEATHER

You have got them about you, somewhere, concealed in your breast there. It will not save you. I tell you I shall have them. I warn you. I don't want to proceed to extreme measures. Give them to me.

(He starts to press desk-button, pauses, and looks at her.) Well?

(Margaret shrugs her shoulders.) (He presses button twice.) I have sent for Dobleman. You have one chance before he comes. Give them to me.

MARGARET

Father, will you believe me just this once? Let me go. I tell you I haven't the documents. I tell you that if you let me leave this room, I shall not carry them away with me. I tell you this on my honor. Do you believe me? Tell me that you do believe

121

me.

STARKWEATHER

I do believe you. You say they are not on you. I believe
you. Now tell me where they are—you have them hidden
somewhere—(Glancing about room.)—And you can go at
once.

(Dobleman enters from right and advances to desk.
Starkweather and Margaret remains silent.)

DOBLEMAN

You rang for me.

STARKWEATHER

(With one last questioning glance at Margaret, who remains
impassive.) Yes, I did. Have you been in that other room all
the time?

DOBLEMAN

Yes, sir.

STARKWEATHER

Did anybody pass through and enter this room?

DOBLEMAN

No, sir.

STARKWEATHER

Very well. We'll see what the maid has to say.

(He presses button once.) Margaret, I give you one last
chance.

MARGARET

I have told you that if I leave this room, I shall not take them with me.

(Maid enters from right rear and advances.)

STARKWEATHER

Has anybody come into this room from the hall in the last few minutes?

Maid

No, sir; not since Mrs. Chalmers came in.

STARKWEATHER

How do you know?

Maid

I was in the hall, sir, dusting all the time.

STARKWEATHER

That will do.

(Maid makes exit to right rear.) Dobleman, a very unusual thing has occurred.

Mrs. Chalmers and I have been alone in this room. Those letters stolen by Gherst had been returned to me by Hubbard but the moment before. They were on my desk. I turned my back for a moment to go to the safe. When I came back they were gone.

DOBLEMAN

(Embarrassed.) Yes, sir.

STARKWEATHER

Mrs. Chalmers took them. She has them now.

DOBLEMAN

(Attempts to speak, stammers.) Er—er—yes, sir

STARKWEATHER

I want them back. What is to be done?

(Dobleman remains in hopeless confusion.) Well!

DOBLEMAN

(Speaking hurriedly and hopefully.) S-send for Mr. Hubbard. He got them for you before.

STARKWEATHER

A good suggestion. Telephone for him. You should find him at the Press Club.

(Dobleman starts to make exit to right.) Don't leave the room. Use this telephone. (Indicating desk telephone.) (Dobleman moves around to left of desk and uses telephone standing up.) From now on no one leaves the room. If my daughter can be guilty of such a theft, it is plain I can trust no one—no one.

DOBLEMAN

(Speaking in transmitter.) Red 6-2-4. Yes, please.

(Waits.)

STARKWEATHER

(Rising.) Call Senator Chalmers as well. Tell him to come immediately.

DOBLEMAN

Yes, sir—immediately.

STARKWEATHER

(Starting to cross stage to center and speaking to Margaret.)
Come over here.

(Margaret follows. She is obedient, frightened, very
subdued—but resolved.)

Why have you done this? Were you truthful when you said
there was nothing between you and this man Knox?

MARGARET

Father; don't discuss this before the—

(Indicating Dobleman.)—the servants.

STARKWEATHER

You should have considered that before you stole the
documents.

(Dobleman, in the meantime, is telephoning in a low voice.)

MARGARET

There are certain dignities—

STARKWEATHER

(Interrupting.) Not for a thief.

(Speaking intensely and in a low voice.) Margaret, it is not
too late. Give them back, and no one shall know.

(A pause, in which Margaret is silent, in the throes of
indecision.)

DOBLEMAN

Mr. Hubbard says he will be here in three minutes. Fortunately, Senator Chalmers is with him.

(Starkweather nods and looks at Margaret.) (Door at left rear opens, and enter Mrs. Starkweather and Connie. They are dressed for the street and evidently just going out.)

MRS. STARKWEATHER

(Speaking in a rush.) We are just going out, Anthony. You were certainly wrong in making us attempt to take that 2:10 train. I simply can't make it. I know I can't. It would have been much wiser—

(Suddenly apprehending the strain of the situation between Starkweather and Margaret.)—Why, what is the matter?

STARKWEATHER

(Patently disturbed by their entrance, speaking to Dobleman, who has finished with the telephone.) Lock the doors.

(Dobleman proceeds to obey.)

MRS. STARKWEATHER

Mercy me! Anthony! What has happened?

(A pause.) Madge! What has happened?

STARKWEATHER

You will have to wait here a few minutes, that is all.

MRS. STARKWEATHER

But I must keep my engagements. And I haven't a minute to spare.

(Looking at Dobleman locking doors.) I do not understand.

STARKWEATHER

(Grimly,) You will, shortly. I can trust no one any more.
When my daughter sees fit to steal—

MRS. STARKWEATHER

Steal!—Margaret! What have you been doing now?

MARGARET

Where is Tommy?

(Mrs. Starkwater is too confounded to answer, and can
only stare from face to face.) (Margaret looks her anxiety to
Connie.)

CONNIE

He is already down in the machine waiting for us. You are
coming, aren't you?

STARKWEATHER

Let him wait in the machine. Margaret will come when I get
done with her.

(A knock is heard at right rear.) (Starkweather looks at
Dobleman and signifies that he is to open door.)

(Dobleman unlocks door, and Hubbabd and Chalmers enter.
Beyond the shortest of nods and recognitions with eyes,
greetings are cut short by the strain that is on all. Dobleman
relocks door.)

STARKWEATHER

(Plunging into it.) Look here, Tom. You know those letters
Gherst stole. Mr. Hubbard recovered them from Knox and
returned them to me this morning. Within five minutes
Margaret stole them from me—here, right in this room. She

has not left the room. They are on her now. I want them.

CHALMERS

(Who is obviously incapable of coping with his wife, and who is panting for breath, his hand pressed to his side.) Madge, is this true?

MARGARET

I haven't them. I tell you I haven't them.

STARKWEATHER

Where are they, then?

(She does not answer.)

If they are in the room we can find them. Search the room. Tom, Mr. Hubbard, Dobleman. They must be recovered at any cost.

(While a thorough search of the room is being made, Mrs. Starkweather, overcome, has Connie assist her to seat at left. Margaret also seats herself, in same chair at desk.)

CHALMERS

(Pausing from search, while others continue.) There is no place to look for them. They are not in the room. Are you sure you didn't mislay them?

STARKWEATHER

Nonsense. Margaret took them. They are a bulky package and not easily hidden. If they aren't in the room, then she has them on her.

CHALMERS

Madge, give them up.

MARGARET

    I haven't them.

    (Chalmers, stepping suddenly up to her, starts feeling for the papers, running his hands over her dress.)

MARGARET

    (Springing to her feet and striking him in the face with her open palm.) How dare you!

    (Chalmers recoils, Mrs. Starkweather is threatened with hysteria and is calmed by the frightened Connie, while Starkweather looks on grimly.)

HUBBARD

    (Giving up search of room.) Possibly it would be better to let me retire, Mr. Starkweather.

STARKWEATHER

    No; those papers are here in this room. If nobody leaves there will be no possible chance for the papers to get out of the room. What would you recommend doing, Hubbard?

HUBBARD

    (Hesitatingly.) Under the circumstances I don't like to suggest—

STARKWEATHER

    Go on.

HUBBARD

    First, I would make sure that she—er—Mrs. Chalmers has taken them.

STARKWEATHER
I have made that certain.

CHALMERS
But what motive could she have for such an act?

(Hubbard looks wise.)

STARKWEATHER
(To Hubbard.) You know more about this than would appear.
What is it?

HUBBARD
I'd rather not. It is too—

(Looks significantly at Mrs. Starkweather and Connie.)—
er—delicate.

STARKWEATHER
This affair has gone beyond all delicacy. What is it?

MARGARET
No! No!

(Chalmers and Starkweather look at her with sudden
suspicion.)

STARKWEATHER
Go on, Mr. Hubbard.

HUBBARD
I'd—I'd rather not.

STARKWEATHER
(Savagely.) I say go on.

HUBBARD

(With simulated reluctance.) Last night—I saw—I was in Knox's rooms—

MARGARET

(Interrupting.) One moment; please. Let him speak, but first send Connie away.

STARKWEATHER

No one shall leave this room till the documents are produced. Margaret, give me the letters, and Connie can leave quietly, and even will Hubbard's lips remain sealed. They will never breathe a word of whatever shameful thing his eyes saw. This I promise you.

(A pause, wherein he waits vainly for Margaret to make a decision.) Go on, Hubbard.

MARGARET

(Who is terror-stricken, and has been wavering.) No! Don't! I'll tell. I'll give you back the documents.

(All are expectant She wavers again, and steels herself to resolution.) No; I haven't them. Say all you have to say.

STARKWEATHER

You see. She has them. She said she would give them back.

(To Hubbard.) Go on.

HUBBARD

Last night—

CONNIE

(Springing up.) I won't stay!

(She rushes to left rear and finds door locked.) Let me out!
Let me out!

MRS. STARKWEATHER
(Moaning and lying back in chair, legs stretched out and
giving preliminary twitches and jerks of hysteria.) I shall die!
I shall die! I know I shall die!

STARKWEATHER
(Sternly, to Connie.) Go back to your mother.

CONNIE
(Returning reluctantly to side of Mrs. Starkweather, sitting
down beside her, and putting fingers in her own ears.) I won't
listen! I won't listen!

STARKWEATHER
(Sternly.) Take your fingers down.

HUBBARD
Hang it all, Chalmers, I wish I were out of this. I don't want
to testify.

STARKWEATHER
Take your fingers down.

(Connie reluctantly removes her fingers.) Now, Hubbard.

HUBBARD
I protest. I am being dragged into this.

CHALMERS
You can't help yourself now. You have cast black suspicions
on my wife.

HUBBARD

All right. She—Mrs. Chalmers visited Knox in his rooms last night.

MRS. STARKWEATHER

(Bursting out.) Oh! Oh! My Madge! It is a lie! A lie! (Kicks violently with her legs.) (Connie soothes her.)

CHALMERS

You've got to prove that, Hubbard. If you have made any mistake it will go hard with you.

HUBBARD

(Indicating Margaret.) Look at her. Ask her.

(Chalmers looks at Margaret with growing suspicion.)

MARGARET

Linda was with me. And Tommy. I had to see Mr. Knox on a very important matter. I went there in the machine. I took Linda and Tommy right into Mr. Knox's room.

CHALMERS

(Relieved.) Ah, that puts a different complexion on it.

HUBBARD

That is not all. Mrs. Chalmers sent the maid and the boy down to the machine and remained.

MARGARET

(Quickly.) But only for a moment

HUBBARD

Much longer—much, much longer. I know how long I was kicking my heels and waiting.

MARGARET

(Desperately.) I say it was but for a moment—a short moment.

STARKWEATHER

(Abruptly, to Hubbard.) Where were you?

HUBBARD

In Knox's bedroom. The fool had forgotten all about me. He was too delighted with his—er—new visitor.

STARKWEATHER

You said you saw.

HUBBARD

The bedroom door was ajar. I opened it.

STARKWEATHER

What did you see?

MARGARET

(Appealing to Hubbard.) Have you no mercy? I say it was only a moment.

(Hubbard shrugs his shoulders.)

STARKWEATHER

We'll settle the length of that moment Tommy is here, and so is the maid. Connie, Margaret's maid is here, isn't she? (Connie does not answer.) Answer me!

CONNIE
Yes.

STARKWEATHER
Dobleman, ring for a maid and tell her to fetch Tommy and
Mrs. Chalmer's maid.

(Dobleman goes to desk and pushes button once.)

MARGARET
No! Not Tommy!

STARKWEATHER
(Looking shrewdly at Margaret, to Dobleman.) Mrs.
Chalmer's maid will do.

(A knock is heard at left rear. Dobleman opens door and
talks to maid. Closes door.)

STARKWEATHER
Lock it.

(Dobleman locks door.)

CHALMERS
(Coming over to Margaret.) So you, the immaculate one,
have been playing fast and loose.

MARGARET
You have no right to talk to me that way, Tom—

CHALMERS
I am your husband.

MARGARET

You have long since ceased being that.

CHALMERS

What do you mean?

MARGARET

I mean just what you have in mind about yourself right now.

CHALMERS

Madge, you are merely conjecturing. You know nothing against me.

MARGARET

I know everything—and without evidence, if you please. I am a woman. It is your atmosphere. Faugh! You have exhaled it for years. I doubt not that proofs, as you would call them, could have been easily obtained. But I was not interested. I had my boy. When he came, I gave you up, Tom. You did not seem to need me any more.

CHALMERS

And so, in retaliation, you took up with this fellow Knox.

MARGARET

No, no. It is not true, Tom. I tell you it is not true.

CHALMERS

You were there, last night, in his rooms, alone—how long we shall soon find out—

(Knock is heard at left rear. Dobleman proceeds to unlock door.) And now you have stolen your father's private papers for your lover.

MARGARET

He is not my lover.

CHALMERS

But you have acknowledged that you have the papers. For whom, save Knox, could you have stolen them?

(Linda enters. She is white and strained, and looks at Margaret for some cue as to what she is to do.)

STARKWEATHER

That is the woman.

(To Linda.) Come here.

(Linda advances reluctantly.) Where were you last night? You know what I mean.

(She does not speak.) Answer me.

LINDA

I don't know what you mean, sir—unless—

STARKWEATHER

Yes, that's it. Go on.

LINDA

But I don't think you have any right to ask me such questions. What if I—if I did go out with my young man—

STARKWEATHER

(To Margaret.) A very faithful young woman you've got.

(Briskly, to the others.) There's nothing to be got out of her. Send for Tommy. Dobleman, ring the bell.

(Dobleman starts to obey.)

MARGARET
(Stopping Dobleman.) No, no; not Tommy. Tell them, Linda.

(Linda looks appealingly at her.)

(Kindly.) Don't mind me. Tell them the truth.

CHALMERS
(Breaking in.) The whole truth.

MARGARET
Yes, Linda, the whole truth.

(Linda, looking very woeful, nerves herself for the ordeal.)

STARKWEATHER
Never mind, Dobleman.

(To Linda.) Very well. You were at Mr. Knox's rooms last night, with your mistress and Tommy.

LINDA
Yes, sir.

STARKWEATHER
Your mistress sent you and Tommy out of the room.

LINDA
Yes, sir.

STARKWEATHER
You waited in the machine.

LINDA

Yes, sir.

STARKWEATHER

(Abruptly springing the point he has been working up to.) How long?

(Linda perceives the gist of the questioning just as she is opening her mouth to reply, and she does not speak.)

MARGARET

(With deliberate calmness of despair.) Half an hour—an hour—any length of time your shameful minds dictate. That will do, Linda. You can go.

STARKWEATHER

No you don't. Stand over there to one side.

(To the others.) The papers are in this room, and I shall keep my mind certain on that point.

HUBBARD

I think I have shown the motive.

CONNIE

You are a beast!

CHALMERS

You haven't told what you saw.

HUBBARD

I saw them in each other's arms—several times. Then I found the stolen documents where Knox had thrown them down. So I pocketed them and closed the door.

CHALMERS
How long after that did they remain together?

HUBBARD
Quite a time, quite a long time.

CHALMERS
And when you last saw them?

HUBBARD
They were in each other's arms—quite enthusiastically, I may say, in each other's arms. (Chalmers is crushed.)

MARGARET
(To Hubbard.) You coward.

(Hubbard smiles.)

(To Starkweather.) When are you going to call off this hound of yours?

STARKWEATHER
When I get the papers. You see what you've been made to pay for them already. Now listen to me closely. Tom, you listen, too. You know the value of these letters. If they are not recovered they will precipitate a turn-over that means not merely money but control and power. I doubt that even you would be re-elected. So what we have heard in this room must be forgotten—absolutely forgotten. Do you understand?

CHALMERS
But it is adultery.

STARKWEATHER

It is not necessary for that word to be mentioned. The point is that everything must be as it was formerly.

CHALMERS

Yes, I understand.

STARKWEATHER

(To Margaret.) You hear. Tom will make no trouble. Now give me the papers. They are mine, you know.

MARGARET

It seems to me the people, who have been lied to, and cajoled, and stolen from, are the rightful owners, not you.

STARKWEATHER

Are you doing this out of love for this—this man, this demagogue?

MARGARET

For the people, the children, the future.

STARKWEATHER

Faugh! Answer me.

MARGARET

(Slowly.) Almost I do not know. Almost I do not know.

(A knock is heard at left rear. Dobleman answers.)

DOBLEMAN

(Looking at card Maid has given him, to Starkweather.) Mr. Rutland.

STARKWEATHER

(Making an impatient gesture, then abruptly changing his mind, speaking grimly.) Very well. Bring him in. I've paid a lot for the Church, now we'll see what the Church can do for me.

CONNIE

(Impulsively crossing stage to Margaret, putting arms around her, and weeping.)

Please, please, Madge, give up the papers, and everything will be hushed up. You heard what father said. Think what it means to me if this scandal comes out. Father will hush it up. Not a soul will dare to breathe a word of it. Give him the papers.

MARGARET

(Kissing her, shaking head, and setting her aside.) No; I can't. But Connie, dearest—

(Connie pauses.) It is not true, Connie. He—he is not my lover. Tell me that you believe me.

CONNIE

(Caressing her.) I do believe you. But won't you return the papers—for my sake?

(A knock at door.)

MARGARET

I can't.

(Enter Rutland.)

(Connie returns to take care of Mrs. Starkweather.)

RUTLAND

(Advances beamingly upon Starkweather.) My, what a family
gathering. I hastened on at once, my dear Mr. Starkweather,
to thank you in person, ere you fled away to New York,
for your generously splendid—yes, generously splendid—
contribution—

(Here the strained situation dawns upon him, and he
remains helplessly with mouth open, looking from one to
another.)

STARKWEATHER

A theft has been committed, Mr. Rutland. My daughter
has stolen something very valuable from me—a package of
private papers, so important—well, if she succeeds in making
them public I shall be injured to such an extent financially
that there won't be any more generously splendid donations
for you or anybody else. I have done my best to persuade her
to return what she has stolen. Now you try. Bring her to a
realization of the madness of what she is doing.

RUTLAND

(Quite at sea, hemming and hawing.) As your spiritual
adviser, Mrs. Chalmers—if this be true—I recommend—I
suggest—I—ahem—I entreat—

MARGARET

Please, Mr. Rutland, don't be ridiculous. Father is only
making a stalking horse out of you. Whatever I may have
done, or not done, I believe I am doing right. The whole
thing is infamous. The people have been lied to and robbed,
and you are merely lending yourself to the infamy of
perpetuating the lying and the robbing. If you persist in
obeying my father's orders—yes, orders—you will lead me
to believe that you are actuated by desire for more of those

generously splendid donations. (Starkweather sneers.)

RUTLAND

(Embarrassed, hopelessly at sea.) This is, I fear—ahem—too delicate a matter, Mr. Starkweather, for me to interfere. I would suggest that it be advisable for me to withdraw— ahem—

STARKWEATHER

(Musingly.) So the Church fails me, too.

(To Rutland.) No, you shall stay right here.

MARGARET

Father, Tommy is down in the machine alone. Won't you let me go?

STARKWEATHER

Give me the papers.

(Mrs. Starkweather rises and totters across to Margaret, moaning and whimpering.)

MRS. STARKWEATHER

Madge, Madge, it can't be true. I don't believe it. I know you have not done this awful thing. No daughter of mine could be guilty of such wickedness. I refuse to believe my ears—

(Mrs. Starkweather sinks suddenly on her knees before Margaret, with clasped hands, weeping hysterically.)

STARKWEATHER

(Stepping to her side.) Get up.

(Hesitates and thinks.) No; go on. She might listen to you.

MARGARET

(Attempting to raise her mother.) Don't, mother, don't. Please get up.

(Mrs. Starkweather resists her hysterically.) You don't understand, mother. Please, please, get up.

MRS. STARKWEATHER

Madge, I, your mother, implore you, on my bended knees. Give up the papers to your father, and I shall forget all I have heard. Think of the family name. I don't believe it, not a word of it; but think of the shame and disgrace. Think of me. Think of Connie, your sister. Think of Tommy. You'll have your father in a terrible state. And you'll kill me. (Moaning and rolling her head.)

I'm going to be sick. I know I am going to be sick.

MARGARET

(Bending over mother and raising her, while Connie comes across stage to help support mother.) Mother, you do not understand. More is at stake than the good name of the family or—(Looking at Rutland.)—God. You speak of Connie and Tommy. There are two millions of Connies and Tommys working as child laborers in the United States to-day. Think of them. And besides, mother, these are all lies you have heard. There is nothing between Mr. Knox and me. He is not my lover. I am not the—the shameful thing—these men have said I am.

CONNIE

(Appealingly.) Madge.

MARGARET

(Appealingly.) Connie. Trust me. I am right. I know I am right.

(Mrs. Starkweather, supported by Connie, moaning incoherently, is led back across stage to chair.)

STARKWEATHER

Margaret, a few minutes ago, when you told me there was nothing between you and this man, you lied to me—lied to me as only a wicked woman can lie.

MARGARET

It is clear that you believe the worst.

STARKWEATHER

There is nothing less than the worst to be believed. Besides, more heinous than your relations with this man is what you have done here in this room, stolen from me, and practically before my very eyes. Well, you have crossed your will with mine, and in affairs beyond your province. This is a man's game in which you are attempting to play, and you shall take the consequences. Tom will apply for a divorce.

MARGARET

That threat, at least, is without power.

STARKWEATHER

And by that means we can break Knox as effectually as by any other. That is one thing the good stupid people will not tolerate in a chosen representative. We will make such a scandal of it—

MRS. STARKWEATHER
(Shocked.) Anthony!

STARKWEATHER
(Glancing irritably at his wife and continuing.) Another
thing. Being proven an adulterous woman, morally unfit for
companionship with your child, your child will be taken
away from you.

MARGARET
No, no. That cannot be. I have done nothing wrong. No
court, no fair-minded judge, would so decree on the evidence
of a creature like that.

(Indicating Hubbard.)

HUBBARD
My evidence is supported. In an adjoining room were two
men. I happen to know, because I placed them there. They
were your father's men at that. There is such a thing as seeing
through a locked door. They saw.

MARGARET
And they would swear to—to anything.

HUBBARD
I doubt not they will know to what to swear.

STARKWEATHER
Margaret, I have told you some, merely some, of the things I
shall do. It is not too late. Return the papers, and everything
will be forgotten.

MARGARET

You would condone this—this adultery. You, who have just said that I was morally unfit to have my own boy, will permit me to retain him. I had never dreamed, father, that your own immorality would descend to such vile depths. Believing this shameful thing of me, you will forgive and forget it all for the sake of a few scraps of paper that stand for money, that stand for a license to rob and steal from the people. Is this your morality—money?

STARKWEATHER

I have my morality. It is not money. I am only a steward; but so highly do I conceive the duties of my stewardship—

MARGARET

(Interrupting, bitterly.) The thefts and lies and all common little sins like adulteries are not to stand in the way of your high duties—that the end hallows the means.

STARKWEATHER

(Shortly.) Precisely.

MARGARET

(To Rutland.) There is Jesuitism, Mr. Rutland. I would suggest that you, as my father's spiritual adviser—

STARKWEATHER

Enough of this foolery. Give me the papers.

MARGARET

I haven't them.

STARKWEATHER

What's to be done, Hubbard?

HUBBARD

> She has them. She has as much as acknowledged that they are not elsewhere in the room. She has not been out of the room. There is nothing to do but search her.

STARKWEATHER

> Nothing else remains to be done. Dobleman, and you, Hubbard, take her behind the screen. Strip her. Recover the papers.

> (Dobleman is in a proper funk, but Hubbard betrays no unwillingness.)

CHALMERS

> No; that I shall not permit. Hubbard shall have nothing to do with this.

MARGARET

> It is too late, Tom. You have stood by and allowed me to be stripped of everything else. A few clothes do not matter now. If I am to be stripped and searched by men, Mr. Hubbard will serve as well as any other man. Perhaps Mr. Rutland would like to lend his assistance.

CONNIE

> Oh, Madge! Give them up.

> (Margaret shakes her head.)

> (To Starkweather.) Then let me search her, father.

STARKWEATHER

> You are too willing. I don't want volunteers. I doubt that I can trust you any more than your sister.

CONNIE
Let mother, then.

STARKWEATHER
(Sneering.) Margaret could smuggle a steamer-trunk of documents past her.

CONNIE
But not the men, father! Not the men!

STARKWEATHER
Why not? She has shown herself dead to all shame.

(Imperatively.) Dobleman!

DOBLEMAN
(Thinking his time has come, and almost dying.) Y-y-yes, sir.

STARKWEATHER
Call in the servants.

MRS. STARKWEATHER
(Crying out in protest.) Anthony!

STARKWEATHER
Would you prefer her to be searched by the men?

MRS. STARKWEATHER
(Subsiding.) I shall die, I shall die. I know I shall die.

STARKWEATHER
Dobleman. Ring for the servants.

(Dobleman, who has been hesitant, crosses to desk and pushes button, then returns toward door.) Send in the maids and the housekeeper.

(Linda, blindly desiring to be of some assistance, starts impulsively toward Margaret.) Stand over there—in the corner.

(Indicating right front.)

(Linda pauses irresolutely and Margaret nods to her to obey and smiles encouragement. Linda, protesting in every fiber of her, goes to right front.)

(A knock at right rear and Dobleman unlocks door, confers with maid, and closes and locks door.)

STARKWEATHER
(To Margaret.) This is no time for trifling, nor for mawkish sentimentality. Return the papers or take the consequences.

(Margaret makes no answer.)

CHALMERS
You have taken a hand in a man's game, and you've got to play it out or quit. Give up the papers.

(Margaret remains resolved and impassive.)

HUBBARD
(Suavely.) Allow me to point out, my dear Mrs. Chalmers, that you are not merely stealing from your father. You are playing the traitor to your class.

STARKWEATHER
And causing irreparable damage.

MARGARET
(Firing up suddenly and pointing to Lincoln's portrait) I doubt not he caused irreparable damage when he freed the slaves and preserved the Union. Yet he recognized no classes. I'd rather be a traitor to my class than to him.

STARKWEATHER
Demagoguery. Demagoguery.

(A knock at right rear. Dobleman opens door. Enter Mrs. Middleton who is the housekeeper, followed by two Housemaids. They pause at rear. Housekeeper to the fore and looking expectantly at Starkweather. The Maids appear timid and frightened.)

HOUSEKEEPER
Yes, sir.

STARKWEATHER
Mrs. Middleton, you have the two maids to assist you. Take Mrs. Chalmers behind that screen there and search her. Strip all her clothes from her and make a careful search. (Maids show perturbation.)

HOUSEKEEPER
(Self-possessed.) Yes, sir. What am I to search for?

STARKWEATHER
Papers, documents, anything unusual. Turn them over to me when you find them.

MARGARET
(In a sudden panic.) This is monstrous! This is monstrous!

STARKWEATHER

So is your theft of the documents monstrous.

MARGARET

(Appealing to the other men, ignoring Rutland and not considering Dobleman at all.)

You cowards! Will you stand by and permit this thing to be done? Tom, have you one atom of manhood in you?

CHALMERS

(Doggedly.) Return the papers, then.

MARGARET

Mr. Rutland—

RUTLAND

(Very awkwardly and oilily.) My dear Mrs. Chalmers. I assure you the whole circumstance is unfortunate. But you are so palpably in the wrong that I cannot interfere— (Margaret turns from him in withering scorn.)—That I cannot interfere.

DOBLEMAN

(Breaking down unexpectedly.) I cannot stand it. I leave your employ, sir. It is outrageous. I resign now, at once. I cannot be a party to this.

(Striving to unlock door.) I am going at once. You brutes! You brutes!

(Breaks into convulsive sobbings.)

CHALMERS

Ah, another lover, I see.

(Dobleman manages to unlock door and starts to open it.)

STARKWEATHER
You fool! Shut that door!

(Dobleman hesitates.) Shut it!

(Dobleman obeys.) Lock it!

(Dobleman obeys.)

MARGARET
(Smiling wistfully, benignantly.) Thank you, Mr. Dobleman.

(To Starkweather.) Father, you surely will not perpetrate this
outrage, when I tell you, I swear to you—

STARKWEATHER
(Interrupting.) Return the documents then.

MARGARET
I swear to you that I haven't them. You will not find them on
me.

STARKWEATHER
You have lied to me about Knox, and I have no reason to
believe you will not lie to me about this matter.

MARGARET
(Steadily.) If you do this thing you shall cease to be my father
forever. You shall cease to exist so far as I am concerned.

STARKWEATHER
You have too much of my own will in you for you ever to
forget whence it came. Mrs. Middleton, go ahead.

(Housekeeper, summoning Maids with her eyes, begins to advance on Margaret.)

CONNIE

(In a passion.) Father, if you do this I shall never speak to you again.

(Breaks down weeping.) (Mrs. Starkweather, during following scene, has mild but continuous shuddering and weeping hysteria.)

STARKWEATHER

(Briskly, looking at watch.) I've wasted enough time on this. Mrs. Middleton, proceed.

MARGARET

(Wildly, backing away from Housekeeper.) I will not tamely submit. I will resist, I promise you.

STARKWEATHER

Use force, if necessary.

(The Maids are reluctant, but Housekeeper commands them with her eyes to close in on Margaret, and they obey.)

(Margaret backs away until she brings up against desk.)

HOUSEKEEPER

Come, Mrs. Chalmers.

(Margaret stands trembling, but refuses to notice Housekeeper.) (Housekeeper places hand on Margaret's arm.)

MARGARET

(Violently flinging the hand off, crying imperiously.) Stand back!

(Housekeeper instinctively shrinks back, as do Maids. But it is only for the moment. They close in upon Margaret to seise her.)

(Crying frantically for help.) Linda! Linda!

(Linda springs forward to help her mistress, but is caught and held struggling by Chalmers, who twists her arm and finally compels her to become quiet.)

(Margaret, struggling and resisting, is hustled across stage and behind screen, the Maids warming up to their work. One of them emerges from behind screen for the purpose of getting a chair, upon which Margaret is evidently forced to sit. The screen is of such height, that occasionally, when standing up and struggling, Margaret's bare arms are visible above the top of it. Muttered exclamations are heard, and the voice of Housekeeper trying to persuade Margaret to submit.)

MARGARET

(Abruptly, piteously.) No! No!

(The struggle becomes more violent, and the screen is overturned, disclosing Margaret seated on chair, partly undressed, and clutching an envelope in her hand which they are trying to force her to relinquish.)

MRS. STARKWEATHER

(Crying wildly.) Anthony! They are taking her clothes off!

(Renewed struggle of Linda with Chalmers at the sight.)

(Starkweather, calling Rutland to his assistance, stands screen up again, then, as an afterthought, pulls screen a little further away from Margaret.)

MARGARET
No! No!

(Housekeeper appears triumphantly with envelope in her hand and hands it to Hubbard.)

HUBBARD
(Immediately.) That's not it.

(Glances at address and starts.) It's addressed to Knox.

STARKWEATHER
Tear it open. Read it.

(Hubbard tears envelope open.) (While this is going on, struggle behind screen is suspended.)

HUBBARD
(Withdrawing contents of envelope.) It is only a photograph—of Mrs. Chalmers.

(Reading.) "For the future—Margaret."

CHALMERS
(Thrusting Linda back to right front and striding up to Hubbard.) Give it to me. (Hubbard passes it to him, and he looks at it, crumples it in his hand, and grinds it under foot.)

STARKWEATHER
That is not what we wanted, Mrs. Middleton. Go on with the search.

(The search goes on behind the screen without any further struggling.) (A pause, during which screen is occasionally agitated by the searchers removing Margaret's garments.)

HOUSEKEEPER
(Appearing around corner of screen.) I find nothing else, sir.

STARKWEATHER
Is she stripped?

HOUSEKEEPER
Yes, sir.

STARKWEATHER
Every stitch?

HOUSEKEEPER
(Disappearing behind screen instead of answering for a pause, during which it is patent that the ultimate stitch is being removed, then reappearing.) Yes, sir.

STARKWEATHER
Nothing?

HOUSEKEEPER
Nothing.

STARKWEATHER
Throw out her clothes—everything.

(A confused mass of feminine apparel is tossed out, falling near Dobleman's feet, who, in consequence, is hugely mortified and embarrassed.)

(Chalmers examines garments, then steps behind screen a moment, and reappears.)

CHALMERS
Nothing.

(Chalmers, Starkweather, and Hubbard gaze at each other dumbfoundedly.)

(The two Maids come out from behind screen and stand near door to right rear.)

(Starkweather is loath to believe, and steps to Margaret's garments and overhauls them.)

STARKWEATHER
(To Chalmers, looking inquiringly toward screen.) Are you sure?

CHALMERS
Yes; I made certain. She hasn't them.

STARKWEATHER
(To Housekeeper.) Mrs. Middleton, examine those girls.

HOUSEKEEPER
(Passing hands over dresses of Maids.) No, sir.

MARGARET
(From behind screen, in a subdued, spiritless voice.) May I dress—now?

(Nobody answers.) It—it is quite chilly.

(Nobody answers.) Will you let Linda come to me, please?

(Starkweather nods savagely to Linda, to obey.) (Linda crosses to garments, gathers them up, and disappears behind screen.)

STARKWEATHER
(To Housekeeper.)

You may go.

(Exit Housekeeper and the two Maids.)

DOBLEMAN
(Hesitating, after closing door.) Shall I lock it? (Starkweather does not answer, and Dobleman leaves door unlocked.)

CONNIE
(Rising.) May I take mother away?

(Starkweather, who is in a brown study, nods.) (Connie assists Mrs. Starkweather to her feet.)

MRS. STARKWEATHER
(Staggering weakly, and sinking back into chair.) Let me rest a moment, Connie. I'll be better. (To Starkweather, who takes no notice.) Anthony, I am going to bed. This has been too much for me. I shall be sick. I shall never catch that train to-day.

(Shudders and sighs, leans head back, closes eyes, and Connie fans her or administers smelling salts.)

CHALMERS
(To Hubbard.) What's to be done?

HUBBARD

(Shrugging shoulders.) I'm all at sea. I had just left the letters with him, when Mrs. Chalmers entered the room. What's become of them? She hasn't them, that's certain.

CHALMERS
But why? Why should she have taken them?

HUBBARD
(Dryly, pointing to crumpled photograph on floor.) It seems very clear to me.

CHALMERS
You think so? You think so?

HUBBARD
I told you what I saw last night at his rooms. There is no other explanation.

CHALMERS
(Angrily.) And that's the sort he is—vaunting his moral superiority—mouthing phrases about theft—our theft—and himself the greatest thief of all, stealing the dearest and sacredest things—

(Margaret appears from behind screen, pinning on her hat. She is dressed, but somewhat in disarray, and Linda follows, pulling and touching and arranging. Margaret pauses near to Rutland, but does not seem to see him.)

RUTLAND
(Lamely.) It is a sad happening—ahem—a sad happening. I am grieved, deeply grieved. I cannot tell you, Mrs. Chalmers, how grieved I am to have been compelled to be present at this—ahem—this unfortunate—

(Margaret withers him with a look and he awkwardly ceases.)

MARGARET
After this, father, there is one thing I shall do—

CHALMERS
(Interrupting.) Go to your lover, I suppose.

MARGARET
(Coldly.) Have it that way if you choose.

CHALMERS
And take him what you have stolen—

STARKWEATHER
(Arousing suddenly from brown study.) But she hasn't them on her. She hasn't been out of the room. They are not in the room. Then where are they?

(During the following, Margaret goes to the door, which Dobleman opens. She forces Linda to go out and herself pauses in open door to listen.)

HUBBARD
(Uttering an exclamation of enlightenment, going rapidly across to window at left and raising it.) It is not locked. It moves noiselessly. There's the explanation.

(To Starkweather.) While you were at the safe, with your back turned, she lifted the window, tossed the papers out to somebody waiting—

(He sticks head and shoulders out of window, peers down, then brings head and shoulders back.)—No; they are not there. Somebody was waiting for them.

STARKWEATHER

But how should she know I had them? You had only just
recovered them?

HUBBARD

Didn't Knox know right away last night that I had taken
them? I took the up-elevator instead of the down when I
heard him running along the hall. Trust him to let her know
what had happened. She was the only one who could recover
them for him. Else why did she come here so immediately
this morning? To steal the package, of course. And she had
some one waiting outside. She tossed them out and closed
the window— (He closes window.)—You notice it makes
no sound.—and sat down again—all while your back was
turned.

STARKWEATHER

Margaret, is this true?

MARGARET

(Excitedly.) Yes, the window. Why didn't you think of it
before? Of course, the window. He—somebody was waiting.
They are gone now—miles and miles away. You will never
get them. They are in his hands now. He will use them in his
speech this afternoon. (Laughs wildly.)

(Suddenly changing her tone to mock meekness, subtle with
defiance.) May I go—now?

(Nobody answers, and she makes exit.) (A moments pause,
during which Starkweather, Chalmers, and Hubbard look at
each other in stupefaction.)

Curtain

ACT IV

SCENE.

Same as Act I. It is half past one of same day. Curtain discloses Knox seated at right front and waiting. He is dejected in attitude.

(Margaret enters from right rear, and advances to him. He rises awkwardly and shakes hands. She is very calm and self-possessed.)

MARGARET

I knew you would come. Strange that I had to send for you so soon after last night—

(With alarm and sudden change of manner.) What is the matter? You are sick. Your hand is cold.

(She warms it in both of her hands.)

KNOX

It is flame or freeze with me.

(Smiling.) And I'd rather flame.

MARGARET

(Becoming aware that she is warming his hand.)

Sit down and tell me what is the matter.

(Leading him by the hand she seats him, at the same time seating herself.)

KNOX

(Abruptly.) After you left last night, Hubbard stole those documents back again.

MARGARET

(Very matter-of-fact.) Yes; he was in your bedroom while I was there.

KNOX

(Startled.) How do you know that? Anyway, he did not know who you were.

MARGARET

Oh yes he did.

KNOX

(Angrily.) And he has dared—?

MARGARET

Yes; not two hours ago. He announced the fact before my father, my mother, Connie, the servants, everybody.

KNOX

(Rising to his feet and beginning to pace perturbedly up and down.) The cur!

MARGARET

(Quietly.) I believe, among other things, I told him he was that myself.

(She laughs cynically.) Oh, it was a pretty family party, I assure you. Mother said she didn't believe it—but that was only hysteria. Of course she believes it—the worst. So does Connie—everybody.

KNOX

(Stopping abruptly and looking at her horror-stricken.) You don't mean they charged——?

MARGARET

No; I don't mean that. I mean more. They didn't charge. They accepted it as a proven fact that I was guilty. That you were my—lover.

KNOX

On that man's testimony?

MARGARET

He had two witnesses in an adjoining room.

KNOX

(Relieved.) All the better. They can testify to nothing more than the truth, and the truth is not serious. In our case it is good, for we renounced each other.

MARGARET

You don't know these men. It is easy to guess that they have been well trained. They would swear to anything.

(She laughs bitterly.) They are my father's men, you know, his paid sleuth-hounds.

KNOX

(Collapsing in chair, holding head in hands, and groaning.)
How you must have suffered. What a terrible time, what a
terrible time! I can see it all—before everybody—your nearest
and dearest. Ah, I could not understand, after our parting
last night, why you should have sent for me today. But now I
know.

MARGARET

No you don't, at all.

KNOX

(Ignoring her and again beginning to pace back and forth,
thinking on his feet.) What's the difference? I am ruined
politically. Their scheme has worked out only too well.
Gifford warned me, you warned me, everybody warned me.
But I was a fool, blind—with a fool's folly. There is nothing
left but you now.

(He pauses, and the light of a new thought irradiates his
face.) Do you know, Margaret, I thank God it has happened
as it has. What if my usefulness is destroyed? There will
be other men—other leaders. I but make way for another.
The cause of the people can never be lost. And though I am
driven from the fight, I am driven to you. We are driven
together. It is fate. Again I thank God for it.

(He approaches her and tries to clasp her in his arms, but she
steps back.)

MARGARET

(Smiling sadly.) Ah, now you flame. The tables are reversed.
Last night it was I. We are fortunate that we choose diverse
times for our moods—else there would be naught but one
sweet melting mad disaster.

167

KNOX

But it is not as if we had done this thing deliberately and selfishly. We have renounced. We have struggled against it until we were beaten. And now we are driven together, not by our doing but Fate's. After this affair this morning there is nothing for you but to come to me. And as for me, despite my best, I am finished. I have failed. As I told you, the papers are stolen. There will be no speech this afternoon.

MARGARET

(Quietly.) Yes there will.

KNOX

Impossible. I would make a triple fool of myself. I would be unable to substantiate my charges.

MARGARET

You will substantiate them. What a chain of theft it is. My father steals from the people. The documents that prove his stealing are stolen by Gherst. Hubbard steals them from you and returns them to my father. And I steal them from my father and pass them back to you.

KNOX

(Astounded.) You?—You?—

MARGARET

Yes; this very morning. That was the cause of all the trouble. If I hadn't stolen them nothing would have happened. Hubbard had just returned them to my father.

KNOX

(Profoundly touched.) And you did this for me—?

168

MARGARET

Dear man, I didn't do it for you. I wasn't brave enough. I should have given in. I don't mind confessing that I started to do it for you, but it soon grew so terrible that I was afraid. It grew so terrible that had it been for you alone I should have surrendered. But out of the terror of it all I caught a wider vision, and all that you said last night rose before me. And I knew that you were right. I thought of all the people, and of the little children. I did it for them, after all. You speak for them. I stole the papers so that you could use them in speaking for the people. Don't you see, dear man?

(Changing to angry recollection.) Do you know what they cost me? Do you know what was done to me, to-day, this morning, in my father's house? I was shamed, humiliated, as I would never have dreamed it possible. Do you know what they did to me? The servants were called in, and by them I was stripped before everybody—my family, Hubbard, the Reverend Mr. Rutland, the secretary, everybody.

KNOX

(Stunned.) Stripped—you?

MARGARET

Every stitch. My father commanded it

KNOX

(Suddenly visioning the scene.) My God!

MARGARET

(Recovering herself and speaking cynically, with a laugh at his shocked face.) No; it was not so bad as that. There was a screen.

(Knox appears somewhat relieved.) But it fell down in the midst of the struggle.

KNOX

But in heaven's name why was this done to you?

MARGARET

Searching for the lost letters. They knew I had taken them.

(Speaking gravely.)

So you see, I have earned those papers. And I have earned the right to say what shall be done with them. I shall give them to you, and you will use them in your speech this afternoon.

KNOX

I don't want them.

MARGARET

(Going to bell and ringing.) Oh yes you do. They are more valuable right now than anything else in the world.

KNOX

(Shaking his head.) I wish it hadn't happened.

MARGARET

(Returning to him, pausing by his chair, and caressing his hair.) What?

KNOX

This morning—your recovering the letters. I had adjusted myself to their loss, and the loss of the fight, and the finding of—you.

(He reaches up, draws down her hand, and presses it to his lips.) So—give them back to your father.

(Margaret draws quickly away from him.) (Enter Man-servant at right rear.)

MARGARET
Send Linda to me.

(Exit Man-servant.)

KNOX
What are you doing?

MARGARET
(Sitting down.) I am going to send Linda for them. They are still in my father's house, hidden, of all places, behind Lincoln's portrait. He will guard them safely, I know.

KNOX
(With fervor.) Margaret! Margaret! Don't send for them. Let them go. I don't want them.

(Rising and going toward her impulsively.) (Margaret rises and retreats, holding him off.) I want you—you—you.

(He catches her hand and kisses it. She tears it away from him, but tenderly.)

MARGARET
(Still retreating, roguishly and tenderly.) Dear, dear man, I love to see you so. But it cannot be.

(Looking anxiously toward right rear.) No, no, please, please sit down.

(Enter Linda from right rear. She is dressed for the street.)

MARGARET
(Surprised.) Where are you going?

LINDA
Tommy and the nurse and I were going down town. There is some shopping she wants to do.

MARGARET
Very good. But go first to my father's house. Listen closely. In the library, behind the portrait of Lincoln—you know it? (Linda nods.)

You will find a packet of papers. It took me five seconds to put it there. It will take you no longer to get it. Let no one see you. Let it appear as though you had brought Tommy to see his grandmother and cheer her up. You know she is not feeling very well just now. After you get the papers, leave Tommy there and bring them immediately back to me. Step on a chair to the ledge of the bookcase, and reach behind the portrait. You should be back inside fifteen minutes. Take the car.

LINDA
Tommy and the nurse are already in it, waiting for me.

MARGARET
Be careful. Be quick.

(Linda nods to each instruction and makes exit.)

KNOX
(Bursting out passionately.) This is madness. You are sacrificing yourself, and me. I don't want them. I want you.

172

I am tired. What does anything matter except love? I have pursued ideals long enough. Now I want you.

MARGARET

(Gravely.) Ah, there you have expressed the pith of it. You will now forsake ideals for me—(He attempts to interrupt.) No, no; not that I am less than an ideal. I have no silly vanity that way. But I want you to remain ideal, and you can only by going on—not by being turned back. Anybody can play the coward and assert they are fatigued. I could not love a coward. It was your strength that saved us last night. I could not have loved you as I do, now, had you been weak last night. You can only keep my love—

KNOX

(Interrupting, bitterly.) By foregoing it—for an ideal. Margaret, what is the biggest thing in the world? Love. There is the greatest ideal of all.

MARGARET

(Playfully.) Love of man and woman?

KNOX

What else?

MARGARET

(Gravely.) There is one thing greater—love of man for his fellowman.

KNOX

Oh, how you turn my preachments back on me. It is a lesson. Nevermore shall I preach. Henceforth—

MARGARET

Yes.

(Chalmers enters unobserved at left, pauses, and looks on.)

KNOX

Henceforth I love. Listen.

MARGARET

You are overwrought. It will pass, and you will see your path straight before you, and know that I am right. You cannot run away from the fight.

KNOX

I can—and will. I want you, and you want me—the man's and woman's need for each other. Come, go with me—now. Let us snatch at happiness while we may.

(He arises, approaches her, and gets her hand in his. She becomes more complaisant, and, instead of repulsing him, is willing to listen and receive.) As I have said, the fight will go on just the same. Scores of men, better men, stronger men, than I, will rise to take my place. Why do I talk this way? Because I love you, love you, love you. Nothing else exists in all the world but love of you.

MARGARET

(Melting and wavering.) Ah, you flame, you flame.

(Chalmers utters an inarticulate cry of rage and rushes forward at Knox)

(Margaret and Knox are startled by the cry and discover Chalmer's presence.)

MARGARET

(Confronting Chalmers and thrusting him slightly back
from Knox, and continuing to hold him off from Knox.) No,
Tom, no dramatics, please. This excitement of yours is only
automatic and conventional. You really don't mean it. You
don't even feel it. You do it because it is expected of you and
because it is your training. Besides, it is bad for your heart.
Remember Dr. West's warning—

(Chalmers, making an unusually violent effort to get at Knox,
suddenly staggers weakly back, signs of pain on his face,
holding a hand convulsively clasped over his heart. Margaret
catches him and supports him to a chair, into which he
collapses.)

CHALMERS

(Muttering weakly.) My heart! My heart!

KNOX

(Approaching.) Can I do anything?

MARGARET

(Calmly.) No; it is all right. He will be better presently.

(She is bending over Chalmers, her hand on his wrist, when
suddenly, as a sign he is recovering, he violently flings her
hand off and straightens up.)

KNOX

(Undecidedly.) I shall go now.

MARGARET

No. You will wait until Linda comes back. Besides, you can't
run away from this and leave me alone to face it.

KNOX

(Hurt, showing that he will stay.) I am not a coward.

CHALMERS

(In a stifled voice that grows stronger.) Yes; wait I have a word for you.

(He pauses a moment, and when he speaks again his voice is all right.)

(Witheringly.) A nice specimen of a reformer, I must say. You, who babbled yesterday about theft. The most high, righteous and noble Ali Baba, who has come into the den of thieves and who is also a thief.

(Mimicking Margaret.) "Ah, you flame, you flame!"

(In his natural voice.) I should call you; you thief, you thief, you wife-stealer, you.

MARGARET

(Coolly.) I should scarcely call it theft.

CHALMERS

(Sneeringly.) Yes; I forgot. You mean it is not theft for him to take what already belongs to him.

MARGARET

Not quite that—but in taking what has been freely offered to him.

CHALMERS

You mean you have so forgotten your womanhood as to offer—

MARGARET

Just that. Last night. And Mr. Knox did himself the honor of refusing me.

KNOX

(Bursting forth.) You see, nothing else remains, Margaret.

CHALMERS

(Twittingly.) Ah, "Margaret."

KNOX

(Ignoring him.) The situation is intolerable.

CHALMERS

(Emphatically). It is intolerable. Don't you think you had better leave this house? Every moment of your presence dishonors it.

MARGARET

Don't talk of honor, Tom.

CHALMERS

I make no excuses for myself. I fancy I never fooled you very much. But at any rate I never used my own house for such purposes.

KNOX

(Springing at him.) You cur!

MARGARET

(Interposing.) No; don't. His heart.

CHALMERS
(Mimicking Margaret.) No dramatics, please.

MARGARET
(Plaintively, looking from one man to the other.) Men are
so strangely and wonderfully made. What am I to do with
the pair of you? Why won't you reason together like rational
human beings?

CHALMERS
(Bitterly gay, rising to his feet.) Yes; let us come and reason
together. Be rational. Sit down and talk it over like civilized
humans. This is not the stone age. Be reassured, Mr. Knox. I
won't brain you. Margaret—

(Indicating chair,) Sit down. Mr. Knox—

(Indicating chair.) Sit down.

(All three seat themselves, in a triangle.) Behold the
problem—the ever ancient and ever young triangle of the
playwright and the short story writer—two men and a
woman.

KNOX
True, and yet not true. The triangle is incomplete. Only one
of the two men loves the woman.

CHALMERS
Yes?

KNOX
And I am that man.

CHALMERS

I fancy you're right.

(Nodding his head.) But how about the woman?

MARGARET

She loves one of the two men.

KNOX

And what are you going to do about it?

CHALMERS

(Judicially.) She has not yet indicated the man.

(Margaret is about to indicate Knox.) Be careful, Madge. Remember who is Tommy's father.

MARGARET

Tom, honestly, remembering what the last years have been can you imagine that I love you?

CHALMERS

I'm afraid I've not—er—not flamed sufficiently.

MARGARET

You have possibly spoken nearer the truth than you dreamed. I married you, Tom, hoping great things of you. I hoped you would be a power for good—

CHALMERS

Politics again. When will women learn they must leave politics alone?

MARGARET

And also, I hoped for love. I knew you didn't love me when we married, but I hoped for it to come.

CHALMERS

And—er—may I be permitted to ask if you loved me?

MARGARET

No; but I hoped that, too, would come.

CHALMERS

It was, then, all a mistake.

MARGARET

Yes; yours, and mine, and my father's.

KNOX

We have sat down to reason this out, and we get nowhere. Margaret and I love each other. Your triangle breaks.

CHALMERS

It isn't a triangle after all. You forget Tommy.

KNOX

(Petulantly.) Make it four-sided, then, but let us come to some conclusion.

CHALMERS

(Reflecting.) Ah, it is more than that. There is a fifth side. There are the stolen letters which Madge has just this morning restolen from her father. Whatever settlement takes place, they must enter into it.

(Changing his tone.) Look here, Madge, I am a fool. Let us talk sensibly, you and Knox and I. Knox, you want my wife. You can have her—on one consideration. Madge, you want Knox. You can have him on one consideration, the same consideration. Give up the letters and we'll forget everything.

MARGARET
Everything?

CHALMERS
Everything. Forgive and forget You know.

MARGARET
You will forgive my—I—this—this adultery?

CHALMERS
(Doggedly.) I'll forgive anything for the letters. I've played fast and loose with you, Madge, and I fancy your playing fast and loose only evens things up. Return the letters and you can go with Knox quietly. I'll see to that. There won't be a breath of scandal. I'll give you a divorce. Or you can stay on with me if you want to. I don't care. What I want is the letters. Is it agreed?

(Margaret seems to hesitate.)

KNOX
(Pleadingly.) Margaret.

MARGARET CHALMERS
(Testily.) Am I not giving you each other? What more do you want? Tommy stays with me. If you want Tommy, then stay with me, but you must give up the letters.

MARGARET

I shall not go with Mr. Knox. I shall not give up the letters. I shall remain with Tommy.

CHALMERS

So far as I am concerned, Knox doesn't count in this. I want the letters and I want Tommy. If you don't give them up, I'll divorce you on statutory grounds, and no woman, so divorced, can keep her child. In any event, I shall keep Tommy.

MARGARET

(Speaking steadily and positively.) Listen, Tom; and you, too, Howard. I have never for a moment entertained the thought of giving up the letters. I may have led you to think so, but I wanted to see just how low, you, Tom, could sink. I saw how low you—all of you—this morning sank. I have learned— much. Where is this fine honor, Tom, which put you on a man-killing rage a moment ago? You'll barter it all for a few scraps of paper, and forgive and forget adultery which does not exist—

(Chalmers laughs skeptically.)—though I know when I say it you will not believe me. At any rate, I shall not give up the letters. Not if you do take Tommy away from me. Not even for Tommy will I sacrifice all the people. As I told you this morning, there are two million Tommys, child-laborers all, who cannot be sacrificed for Tommy's sake or anybody's sake.

(Chalmers shrugs his shoulders and smiles in ridicule.)

KNOX

Surely, Margaret, there is a way out for us. Give up the letters. What are they?—only scraps of paper. Why match them against happiness—our happiness?

MARGARET

But as you told me yourself, those scraps of paper represent the happiness of millions of lives. It is not our happiness that is matched against some scraps of paper. It is our happiness against millions of lives—like ours. All these millions have hearts, and loves, and desires, just like ours.

KNOX

But it is a great social and cosmic process. It does not depend on one man. Kill off, at this instant, every leader of the people, and the process will go on just the same. The people will come into their own. Theft will be unseated. It is destiny. It is the process. Nothing can stop it.

MARGARET

But it can be retarded.

KNOX

You and I are no more than straws in relation to it. We cannot stop it any more than straws can stop an ocean tide. We mean nothing—except to each other, and to each other we mean all the world.

MARGARET

(Sadly and tenderly.) All the world and immortality thrown in.

CHALMERS

(Breaking in.) Nice situation, sitting here and listening to a strange man woo my wife in terms of sociology and scientific slang.

(Both Margaret and Knox ignore him.)

KNOX

Dear, I want you so.

MARGARET

(Despairingly.) Oh! It is so hard to do right!

KNOX

(Eagerly.) He wants the letters very badly. Give them up for Tommy. He will give Tommy for them.

CHALMERS

No; emphatically no. If she wants Tommy she can stay on; but she must give up the letters. If she wants you she may go; but she must give up the letters.

KNOX

(Pleading for a decision.) Margaret.

MARGARET

Howard. Don't tempt me and press me. It is hard enough as it is.

CHALMERS

(Standing up.) I've had enough of this. The thing must be settled, and I leave it to you, Knox. Go on with your love-making. But I won't be a witness to it. Perhaps I—er—retard the—er—the flame process. You two must make up your minds, and you can do it better without me. I am going to get a drink and settle my nerves. I'll be back in a minute.

(He moves toward exit to right.) She will yield, Knox. Be warm, be warm.

(Pausing in doorway.) Ah, you flame! Flame to some purpose. (Exit Chalmers.)

(Knox rests his head despairingly on his hand, and Margaret, pausing and looking at him sadly for a moment, crosses to him, stands beside him, and caresses his hair.)

MARGARET

It is hard, I know, dear. And it is hard for me as well.

KNOX

It is so unnecessary.

MARGARET

No, it is necessary. What you said last night, when I was weak, was wise. We cannot steal from my child—

KNOX

BUT IF HE GIVES YOU TOMMY? MARGARET

(Shaking her head.) Nor can we steal from any other woman's child—from all the children of all the women. And other things I heard you say, and you were right. We cannot live by ourselves alone. We are social animals. Our good and our ill—all is tied up with all humanity.

KNOX

(Catching her hand and caressing it.) I do not follow you. I hear your voice, but I do not know a word you say. Because I am loving your voice—and you. I am so filled with love that there is no room for anything else. And you, who yesterday were so remote and unattainable, are so near and possible, so immediately possible. All you have to do is to say the word, one little word. Say it.—Say it.

(He carries her hand to his lips and holds it there.)

MARGARET
(Wistfully.) I should like to. I should like to. But I can't.

KNOX
You must.

MARGARET
There are other and greater things that say must to me. Oh, my dear, have you forgotten them? Things you yourself have spoken to me—the great stinging things of the spirit, that are greater than you and I, greater even than our love.

KNOX
I exhaust my arguments—but still I love you.

MARGARET
And I love you for it.

(Chalmers enters from right, and sees Margaret still caressing Knox's hair.)

CHALMERS
(With mild elation, touched with sarcasm.) Ah, I see you have taken my advice, and reached a decision.

(They do not answer. Margaret moves slowly away and seats herself.) (Knox remains with head bowed on hand.) No?

(Margaret shakes her head.) Well, I've thought it over, and I've changed my terms. Madge, go with Knox, take Tommy with you.

(Margaret wavers, but Knox, head bowed on hand, does not see her.) There will be no scandal. I'll give you a proper divorce. And you can have Tommy.

KNOX

(Suddenly raising his head, joyfully, pleadingly.) Margaret!

(Margaret is swayed, but does not speak.)

CHALMERS

You and I never hit it off together any too extraordinarily well, Madge; but I'm not altogether a bad sort. I am easy-going. I always have been easy-going. I'll make everything easy for you now. But you see the fix I am in. You love another man, and I simply must regain those letters. It is more important than you realize.

MARGARET

(Incisively.) You make me realize how important those letters are.

KNOX

Give him the letters, Margaret

CHALMERS

So she hasn't turned them over to you yet?

MARGARET

No; I still have them.

KNOX

Give them to him.

CHALMERS
Selling out for a petticoat. A pretty reformer.

KNOX
(Proudly.)

A better lover.

MARGARET
(To Chalmers.)

He is weak to-day. What of it? He was strong last night. He
will win back his strength again. It is human to be weak.
And in his very weakness now, I have my pride, for it is the
weakness of love. God knows I have been weak, and I am not
ashamed of it. It was the weakness of love. It is hard to stifle
one's womanhood always with morality. (Quickly.)

But do not mistake, Tom. This of mine is no conventional
morality. I do not care about nasty gossipy tongues and
sensation-mongering sheets; nor do I care what any persons
of all the persons I know, would say if I went away with Mr.
Knox this instant. I would go, and go gladly and proudly
with him, divorce or no divorce, scandal or scandal triple-
fold—if—if no one else were hurt by what I did. (To Knox.)

Howard, I tell you that I would go with you now, in all
willingness and joy, with May-time and the songs of all
singing birds in my heart—were it not for the others. But
there is a higher morality. We must not hurt those others. We
dare not steal our happiness from them. The future belongs
to them, and we must not, dare not, sacrifice that future nor
give it in pledge for our own happiness. Last night I came to
you. I was weak—yes; more than that—I was ignorant. I did
not know, even as late as last night, the monstrous vileness,
the consummate wickedness of present-day conditions. I

learned that today, this morning, and now. I learned that
the morality of the Church was a pretense. Far deeper than
it, and vastly more powerful, was the morality of the dollar.
My father, my family, my husband, were willing to condone
what they believed was my adultery. And for what? For a few
scraps of paper that to them represented only the privilege to
plunder, the privilege to steal from the people.

(To Chalmers.) Here are you, Tom, not only willing and
eager to give me into the arms of the man you believe my
lover, but you throw in your boy—your child and mine—to
make it good measure and acceptable. And for what? Love
of some woman?—any woman? No. Love of humanity?
No. Love of God? No. Then for what? For the privilege of
perpetuating your stealing from the people—money, bread
and butter, hats, shoes, and stockings—for stealing all these
things from the people.

(To Knox.) Now, and at last, do I realize how stern and awful
is the fight that must be waged—the fight in which you and
I, Howard, must play our parts and play them bravely and
uncomplainingly—you as well as I, but I even more than
you. This is the den of thieves. I am a child of thieves. All
my family is composed of thieves. I have been fed and reared
on the fruits of thievery. I have been a party to it all my life.
Somebody must cease from this theft, and it is I. And you
must help me, Howard.

CHALMERS
(Emitting a low long whistle.) Strange that you never went
into the suffragette business. With such speech-making
ability you would have been a shining light.

KNOX
(Sadly.) The worst of it is, Margaret, you are right. But it
is hard that we cannot be happy save by stealing from the

happiness of others. Yet it hurts, deep down and terribly, to forego you. (Margaret thanks him with her eyes.)

CHALMERS

(Sarcastically.) Oh, believe me, I am not too anxious to give up my wife. Look at her. She's a pretty good woman for any man to possess.

MARGARET

Tom, I'll accept a quiet divorce, marry Mr. Knox, and take Tommy with me—on one consideration.

CHALMERS

And what is that?

MARGARET

That I retain the letters. They are to be used in his speech this afternoon.

CHALMERS

No they're not.

MARGARET

Whatever happens, do whatever worst you can possibly do, that speech will be given this afternoon. Your worst to me will be none too great a price for me to pay.

CHALMERS

No letters, no divorce, no Tommy, nothing.

MARGARET

Then will you compel me to remain here. I have done nothing wrong, and I don't imagine you will make a scandal.

(Enter Linda at right rear, pausing and looking inquiringly.) There they are now.

(To Linda.) Yes; give them to me.

(Linda, advancing, draws package of documents from her breast. As she is handing them to Margaret, Chalmers attempts to seise them.)

KNOX
(Springing forward and thrusting Chalmers back.) That you shall not!

(Chalmers is afflicted with heart-seizure, and staggers.)

MARGARET
(Maternally, solicitously.) Tom, don't! Your heart! Be careful!

(Chalmers starts to stagger toward bell) Howard! Stop him! Don't let him ring, or the servants will get the letters away from us. (Knox starts to interpose, but Chalmers, growing weaker, sinks into a chair, head thrown back and legs out straight before him.) Linda, a glass of water.

(Linda gives documents to Margaret, and makes running exit to right rear.) (Margaret bends anxiously over Chalmers.) (A pause.)

KNOX
(Touching her hand.) Give them to me.

(Margaret gives him the documents, which he holds in his hand, at the same time she thanks him with her eyes.) (Enter Linda with glass of water, which she hands to Margaret.) (Margaret tries to place the glass to Chalmer's lips.)

CHALMERS
(Dashing the glass violently from her hand to the floor and speaking in smothered voice.) Bring me a whiskey and soda.

(Linda looks at Margaret interrogatively. Margaret is undecided what to say, shrugs her shoulders in helplessness, and nods her head.)

(Linda makes hurried exit to right.)

MARGARET
(To Knox.) You will go now and you will give the speech.

KNOX
(Placing documents in inside coat pocket.) I will give the speech.

MARGARET
And all the forces making for the good time coming will be quickened by your words. Let the voices of the millions be in it.

(Chalmers, legs still stretched out, laughs cynically.)

You know where my heart lies. Some day, in all pride and honor, stealing from no one, hurting no one, we shall come together—to be together always.

KNOX
(Drearily.) And in the meantime?

MARGARET
We must wait

KNOX

(Decidedly.) We will wait.

CHALMERS

(Straightening up.) For me to die? eh?

(During the following speech Linda enters from right with whiskey and soda and gives it to Chalmers, who thirstily drinks half of it. Margaret dismisses Linda with her eyes, and Linda makes exit to right rear.)

KNOX

I hadn't that in mind, but now that you mention it, it seems to the point. That heart of yours isn't going to carry you much farther. You have played fast and loose with it as with everything else. You are like the carter who steals hay from his horse that he may gamble. You have stolen from your heart. Some day, soon, like the horse, it will quit We can afford to wait. It won't be long.

CHALMERS

(After laughing incredulously and sipping his whiskey.) Well, Knox, neither of us wins. You don't get the woman. Neither do I. She remains under my roof, and I fancy that is about all. I won't divorce her. What's the good? But I've got her tied hard and fast by Tommy. You won't get her.

(Knox, ignoring hint, goes to right rear and pauses in doorway.)

MARGARET

Work. Bravely work. You are my knight. Go.

(Knox makes exit.)

(Margaret stands quietly, face averted from audience and turned toward where Knox was last to be seen.)

CHALMERS
Madge.

(Margaret neither moves nor answers.) I say, Madge.

(He stands up and moves toward her, holding whiskey glass in one hand.) That speech is going to make a devil of a row. But I don't think it will be so bad as your father says. It looks pretty dark, but such things blow over. They always do blow over. And so with you and me. Maybe we can manage to forget all this and patch it up somehow.

(She gives no sign that she is aware of his existence.) Why don't you speak? (Pause.)

(He touches her arm.) Madge.

MARGARET
(Turning upon him in a blase of wrath and with unutterable loathing.)

Don't touch me!

(Chalmers recoils.)

Curtain

Printed in Great Britain
by Amazon

84162655R10112